Military Families

Other Books in the Current Controversies Series

Military Families

Sylvia Engdahl, Book Editor

GREENHAVEN PRESS
A part of Gale, Cengage Learning

Farmington Hills, Mich • San Francisco • New York • Waterville, Maine
Meriden, Conn • Mason, Ohio • Chicago

Elizabeth Des Chenes, *Director, Content Strategy*
Cynthia Sanner, *Publisher*
Douglas Dentino, *Manager, New Product*

© 2014 Greenhaven Press, a part of Gale, Cengage Learning

WCN: 01-100-101

LIBRARY OF CONGRESS CATALOGING-IN-PUBLICATION DATA

Engdahl, Sylvia.
  Military families / Sylvia Engdahl, book editor.
    pages cm. -- (Current controversies)
  Includes bibliographical references and index.
  ISBN 978-0-7377-6878-7 (hardcover) -- ISBN 978-0-7377-6879-4 (pbk.)
  1. Families of military personnel--United States--Social conditions. 2. Families of military personnel--Services for--United States--Evaluation. 3. Soldiers--United States--Pay, allowances, etc. 4. Soldiers--United States--Social conditions. 5. Soldiers--Services for--United States--Evaluation. I. Title.
  UB403.E34 2013
  355.1'20973--dc23
                    2013041402

Printed in the United States of America
1 2 3 4 5 6 7 18 17 16 15 14

Contents

Chapter 1: Do Rising Costs Justify Reducing Benefits to Military Families?

Yes: Rising Costs Justify Reducing Benefits to Military Families

A veteran argues that military pay needs to be cut because the cost is becoming too high. The number of enlisted service members will be reduced to allow for increases in officers' pay, and enlisted soldiers too are paid more than many civilians when allowances for housing, meals, and clothing are taken into account; the Army even pays child support for divorced soldiers.

No: Rising Costs Do Not Justify Reducing Benefits to Military Families

A widely read article on the Internet (the first viewpoint in this chapter) drew a storm of protest from military families; within days of its appearance, thirty pages of comments were posted, and later the number doubled. It was pointed out that some of its figures were inaccurate and, moreover, it ignored military families' increased child care costs and the expense of frequent moves.

The inaccuracies in a widely read Internet article (the first viewpoint in this chapter) claiming that military benefits are excessive presents a false picture and is insulting to service members and veterans. Military duties demand high skill and involve extreme sacrifice on the part of families who are left alone for long periods, as well as on that of many veterans who cannot find work or are permanently injured as a result of their military service.

Military families experience great stress because of the financial problems resulting from deployments, frequent relocations, and the inability of spouses to find jobs after moving. More than a third of them have trouble paying monthly bills, and many are heavily in debt. When people are asked to serve their country it should not result in poverty for their families.

Chapter 2: What Personal and Social Problems Do Military Families Face?

The children of military families frequently attend seven to nine different schools before they graduate from high school, which produces additional stress along with that of a parent's absence during deployment. Children often show signs of stress such as fear, irritability, and aggression, while teens tend to become rebellious. Communities—especially public schools—need to understand these problems and provide more support.

No: Being Part of a Military Family Is Not Detrimental to Children

Military children have many admirable qualities: their
sense of humor, their service to the community, their
loyalty to their military parents, their patriotism, their
support of each other, their adaptability, their compassion, their global knowledge, their strength in the face of
challenges, and the fact that they, too, serve their country
by giving their parents peace of mind.

Chapter 4: What Is the Government Doing to Help Military Families?

Military Morale, Welfare, and Recreation (MWR) programs promote leisure activities such as sports, fitness, cultural arts, travel, and other forms of recreation with the aim of improving quality of life for service members and their families. They also provide child care and programs for youth through high school age.

US Air Force

The military services offer many activities to children and teens of military personnel. For example, among the Air Force programs available to teens are a teen council, teen leadership camp, aviation camp, space camp, Sideline Sports camp, a kids' run, Operation Purple camps, high adventure camps, and many opportunities in the performing arts.

Foreword

By definition, controversies are "discussions of questions in which opposing opinions clash" (*Webster's Twentieth Century Dictionary Unabridged*). Few would deny that controversies are a pervasive part of the human condition and exist on virtually every level of human enterprise. Controversies transpire between individuals and among groups, within nations and between nations. Controversies supply the grist necessary for progress by providing challenges and challengers to the status quo. They also create atmospheres where strife and warfare can flourish. A world without controversies would be a peaceful world; but it also would be, by and large, static and prosaic.

The Series' Purpose

The purpose of the Current Controversies series is to explore many of the social, political, and economic controversies dominating the national and international scenes today. Titles selected for inclusion in the series are highly focused and specific. For example, from the larger category of criminal justice, Current Controversies deals with specific topics such as police brutality, gun control, white collar crime, and others. The debates in Current Controversies also are presented in a useful, timeless fashion. Articles and book excerpts included in each title are selected if they contribute valuable, long-range ideas to the overall debate. And wherever possible, current information is enhanced with historical documents and other relevant materials. Thus, while individual titles are current in focus, every effort is made to ensure that they will not become quickly outdated. Books in the Current Controversies series will remain important resources for librarians, teachers, and students for many years.

In addition to keeping the titles focused and specific, great care is taken in the editorial format of each book in the series. Book introductions and chapter prefaces are offered to provide background material for readers. Chapters are organized around several key questions that are answered with diverse opinions representing all points on the political spectrum. Materials in each chapter include opinions in which authors clearly disagree as well as alternative opinions in which authors may agree on a broader issue but disagree on the possible solutions. In this way, the content of each volume in Current Controversies mirrors the mosaic of opinions encountered in society. Readers will quickly realize that there are many viable answers to these complex issues. By questioning each author's conclusions, students and casual readers can begin to develop the critical thinking skills so important to evaluating opinionated material.

Current Controversies is also ideal for controlled research. Each anthology in the series is composed of primary sources taken from a wide gamut of informational categories including periodicals, newspapers, books, US and foreign government documents, and the publications of private and public organizations. Readers will find factual support for reports, debates, and research papers covering all areas of important issues. In addition, an annotated table of contents, an index, a book and periodical bibliography, and a list of organizations to contact are included in each book to expedite further research.

Perhaps more than ever before in history, people are confronted with diverse and contradictory information. During the Persian Gulf War, for example, the public was not only treated to minute-to-minute coverage of the war, it was also inundated with critiques of the coverage and countless analyses of the factors motivating US involvement. Being able to sort through the plethora of opinions accompanying today's major issues, and to draw one's own conclusions, can be a complicated and frustrating struggle. It is the editors' hope that Current Controversies will help readers with this struggle.

Introduction

> *"Children in military families make sacrifices and serve their country as much as anyone in uniform does. . . . In so many loving ways, our children quietly shoulder part of the burden, making their mom or dad understand that what they are doing is important."*

Most Americans respect and appreciate the service of military men and women to the nation and recognize the magnitude of the sacrifices service members make, especially when deployed during time of war. The majority of citizens, however, are not aware of the ongoing challenges faced by military families. That the separation imposed by deployment takes a toll on family members is obvious, as is the grief they experience when dealing with a loved one's injury or death. But the day-to-day life of military families while together also involves hardships that are not shared by others.

To begin with, few military families have permanent homes. Generally, service members are transferred to a different location every two or three years, or even more often, on short notice and with little if any choice as to where they will go. In military terminology such a transfer is known as a Permanent Change of Station, or PCS, although it is "permanent" only in the sense that they will not return to the home they are leaving. A PCS means packing up all personal belongings and moving to an unfamiliar area. If the family owns a house, they must sell it, sometimes at a loss; and finding a place to live in the new area may be difficult—in many cases they must settle for temporary living quarters. They must leave all of their friends behind and make new ones. The children must leave their schools, dropping out of whatever extracurricular activities are important to them, and enter new schools in the middle of the year when it may be hard to catch up with the classes in which they are placed. And then, in another three years at most, they must go through the same process all over again.

It is common for military kids (or "military brats," the term children of career service members traditionally use for themselves) to attend six to nine different schools between kindergarten and graduating from high school. They sometimes have trouble transferring credits or retaining athletic eligibility. Since academic requirements differ from state to state, graduation may even be delayed.

While transfers are difficult for kids and teens, they are often even more so for the civilian spouse of a service member, who may have trouble finding a job in their new location. Many occupations, such as teaching or nursing, require a state license that cannot be quickly obtained. A military spouse successful in his or her career may be unable to continue it in a different state; he or she may not be able to get work at all, even if the family is badly in need of income. It may be impossible to arrange for childcare. And of course adults, too, must say goodbye to their friends when they move, knowing they may never see them again—just as they may rarely, if ever, see their own parents and extended families.

Life at a military base or post differs in many ways from life outside. Some families live in base housing, while others live off-base, depending on their preferences and the availability of accommodations; but all of them are in close contact with their bases, which are self-contained communities with their own shopping and recreational and medical facilities, as well as their own police. Social life is centered on official FRGs (Family Readiness Groups) and other base support organizations. Shopping at military commissaries and exchanges—on-base stores where prices are lower than elsewhere—is a necessity, considering that military pay, except for high-ranking officers, is often barely sufficient to meet a family's needs. Medical care and admission to theaters, pools, sports facilities, and so forth is free, but only for service members' dependents with official ID cards, which must be shown on entering the base and for every service obtained there. Furthermore, military bases have strict rules and customs regarding conduct, and the military culture fosters conformity. Some family members enjoy the sense of community this provides, while others find it uncomfortably restrictive. Either way, they are bound by it. Since a service member is not free to choose a different lifestyle, neither is his or her family.

Along with these problems comes the stress caused by deployment, during which one parent must take full responsibility for the family's welfare while the other is absent. At a time of loneliness and worry, the parent left without a partner to share the tasks of home maintenance and child rearing bears a heavy load, part of which may be assumed by older children and teens. "Children in military families make sacrifices and serve their country as much as anyone in uniform does," said Marine General Peter Pace, the chairman of the Joint Chiefs of Staff, in an April 2006 interview. "In so many loving ways, our children quietly shoulder part of the burden, making their mom or dad understand that what they are doing is important."

According to the Department of Defense, as of 2011, counting both active and reserve forces, there were nearly two million US military children, 25 percent of whom were teens. Including families no longer in the military, more than two million children have had a parent deploy to Iraq or Afghanistan, and twenty-two hundred have lost a parent there, while at least nineteen thousand have had a parent wounded in action.

Not all military children have even one parent living at home. In 2011, there were forty thousand active-duty military families in which both parents were service members and about seventy-five thousand single-parent families—meaning that their children, plus those of over eighty thousand similarly situated reservists, must go to live with grandparents or other relatives if their parents are deployed.

Whatever the circumstances, for most families missing the absent member and fearing for his or her safety is the worst aspect of deployment. So it would seem that the service member's homecoming would be a time of undiluted joy. But this is not always the case. Many individuals have serious problems after returning from a combat assignment. The experiences they have undergone have often changed them, so that readjustment to normal life is difficult; they may seem like different people to their families even if they are in good health—and certainly if they are not. Family members, too, have been changed by the extra responsibilities they have taken on. The reintegration of the family may take a while. Moreover, because multiple deployments are now common, anticipation of the next absence may interfere with enjoyment of the time spent at home.

Yet despite all these difficulties, the majority of military families adjust well to their lifestyle. It has advantages in addition to the stability provided by a supportive community, including free health care and the service member's steady job. Moving to new locales can be viewed as an adventure. Some families have the opportunity to travel to other parts of the world and reside in different countries. Whether or not this happens, they meet a wide variety of people from diverse backgrounds and become able to adapt easily to changing situations. They have a chance to learn first-hand about things the average person may never even read about. And many organizations offer activities for military kids, such as camps and scholarships, that are not open to others.

"The military culture is so unique that being a part of it makes you feel kind of special," explains the National Military Family Association booklet *What Military Teens Want You to*

Know. "Throw in terms like 'American hero' and it's easy to see why teens say they are proud of the job their parents do for the country. . . . Military teens overwhelmingly name their military parent as a positive role model."

Pride in serving and safeguarding the nation is at the heart of the military culture, and it is shared by spouses and children as well as by those in uniform. "We owe each day of security and freedom that we enjoy to the members of our Armed Forces and their families," President Barack Obama said in his 2010 proclamation of Military Family Month. "Behind our brave service men and women, there are family members and loved ones who share in their sacrifice and provide unending support. . . . Across America, military families inspire us all with their courage, strength, and deep devotion to our country."

CHAPTER 1

Do Rising Costs Justify Reducing Benefits to Military Families?

Chapter Preface

In the past, military pay was relatively low, but in recent decades, since the end of the Vietnam War (1975) and the establishment of an all-volunteer military force (1973), it has risen steadily because of the need to boost recruitment. The cost of pay and benefits increased by 90 percent between 2001 and 2013. Since 2010 there has been, on average, no significant gap between military compensation and that of civilians for people with equal levels of experience and education when housing allowances, free medical care, and tax benefits are figured in. In some cases it has even exceeded it.

But military personnel costs have risen so much that they now consume a large percentage of the total military budget, and experts fear that in the near future there may not be enough money to maintain the ships, planes, and other equipment service members need to accomplish their mission. "We are on an unsustainable course," Arnold Punaro, a retired Marine major general who chairs the Reserve Forces Policy Board, told *The Washington Post*. "We are trading off active-duty combat readiness to protect all of these benefits."

So when in 2013 it became known that the military would have to cut back spending unless Congress took action, there were proposals to reduce personnel expenditures such as pay raises and retirement benefits. Some people argued that military compensation is unreasonably high in comparison to civilian income, especially for enlisted men and women without families, considering that most service members not deployed to combat areas do work that involves no hardship. And it was pointed out that many young military families who have trouble making ends meet simply don't know how to manage money—for instance, some drive expensive cars they cannot afford.

These proposals were not well received by the public. Military spouses vehemently protested that the critics did not understand the hidden costs incurred by military families, who are required to move to a different area every two or three years: for example, the frequent inability to break even on the sale of their homes; the temporary—or sometimes permanent—loss of spousal income and/or increased childcare expense; and generally some out-of-pocket moving expenses beyond those that are reimbursed. More fundamentally, service members must do whatever work they are assigned and during their term of enlistment cannot quit; even when not deployed, they must be ready for deployment at any moment. What other job can demand that a person leave his or her family without notice and go into danger, far from loved ones?

Moreover, it is recognized that to raise armed forces composed entirely of volunteers it is necessary to offer generous benefits, not only to recruit but to encourage service members to reenlist in order to retain the highly trained personnel the military needs. Indeed, because of the advanced technical nature of today's military jobs, too much personnel turnover drives training expenses up, to the point that the money spent on reenlistment inducements is viewed as a smart investment rather than a net expense. A 2012 congressional study found that there is currently no problem recruiting or retaining qualified service members, but that might not be the case if compensation were significantly reduced—and the only alternative to attracting enough volunteers is to go back to a draft.

Most Americans strongly support the nation's troops and believe they deserve as much compensation as it is possible to provide. It is widely felt that reducing benefits would be perceived as a lack of support, and therefore any attempt to do so would be politically unpopular. In August 2013, President Barack Obama announced that military pay will be exempted from automatic across-the-board defense spending cuts for at least another year. How the problem of rising costs is solved in the future will depend on the US Congress.

Defense Budget Faces Cuts to Personnel After Decade of War

David Wood

David Wood is a Pulitzer Prize-winning journalist who has been a staff correspondent for Time, the Los Angeles Times, *and the* Baltimore Sun, *among other media.*

For more than a decade, Congress and the Pentagon have spent money on the nation's 1.3 million active-duty troops and their families. Salaries and benefits soared far above civilian compensation, military bases and housing were refurbished, support services like day care, family counseling and on-base college courses were expanded.

Now comes the reckoning. These personnel costs, necessary and warranted for those bearing the burden of war, are threatening to wreck the military, squeezing the accounts meant to fix or replace gear worn from a decade of war, for research and development, and for new missions in, say, Africa.

So stubbornly are personnel costs rising that at the current rate of increase, they would consume the entire defense budget by the year 2039, leaving well-paid troops standing around with their tanks, ships and airplanes rusting and out of gas.

The problem has been evident for years—the past two defense secretaries have called personnel costs "unsustainable." But neither the [Barack] Obama White House nor Congress has signalled its willingness to tackle the issue by proposing bold reductions in pay and benefits—or by deep cuts in the active-duty force.

In his confirmation hearing Thursday [January 31, 2013], former Sen. Chuck Hagel (R-Neb.) will get a chance to weigh in on the issue as the nominee for defense secretary. He has said nothing in public on the issue, and his background gives little clue: as a successful businessman he's cognizant of the bottom line; as a former combat infantryman, his heart may make him too reluctant to touch the grunts' pay stubs.

Cost-Cutting May Not Be Done Wisely

But with deep cuts in defense spending barrelling down toward the Pentagon, some defense officials and outside experts fear that the opportunity for thoughtful reforms may be passing. Personnel costs are likely to be cut—but perhaps not wisely. A freeze on hiring of new civilian personnel, for instance, could demolish plans to hire more mental health care providers for returning troops suffering from post-traumatic stress, even though Ash Carter, deputy defense secretary, has vowed to protect such programs "to the extent feasible."

Since 2001, total military compensation, including pay and benefits, grew by 20.5 percent, while comparable private-sector civilian pay did not increase at all.

Military pay and benefits "are the third rail of budget planning in the Defense Department," said Gordon Adams, a defense economist who oversaw the post-Cold War defense drawdown (1990s) during the [Bill] Clinton administration. With no long-term budget deal in sight and no long-term planning in the works, the shrinking of the Defense Department "will happen year by year—more ankle-biting than systematic planning," Adams said.

Pentagon spending plans are getting slammed by the automatic cuts under sequestration, scheduled to take place on March 1 [2013], by the likelihood that Congress will pass no new defense spending bill, leaving the Pentagon confined, under a continuing resolution to last year's defense budget plan; and by long-term spending cuts which have yet to be made.

But the impact is real. The Pentagon has been spending money it expected from the 2013 budget proposed last year by the White House. Cranking back to conform to last year's budget levels will be painful, Army Chief of Staff Gen. Ray Odierno said recently, requiring the Army to squeeze $6 billion out of its operations and maintenance accounts by Oct. 1. These are funds that pay for fuel, training, some family support programs and vehicle maintenance.

And while Pentagon officials have vowed not to cut family programs, a continuing resolution, rather than a new 2013 budget, will not allow the Army to move money from one operations account to another—it all gets cut, Odierno said.

"People have been in denial about this ongoing trend, and now the accumulated impact of it is coming home," said Clark Murdock, a former senior planner at the Pentagon and a senior analyst at the Center for Strategic and International Studies, a Washington think tank.

Military Pay Has Risen Faster than Civilian Pay

But the data is clear. Since 2001, total military compensation, including pay and benefits, grew by 20.5 percent, while comparable private-sector civilian pay did not increase at all, according to a broad Pentagon review of pay and compensation released last year. The cost of military compensation rose steeply even though the size of the active-duty force grew by only 3 percent during that period.

Part of the reason was that Congress mandated that military personnel should get an annual pay raise 1 to 1.5 percent higher than the Employment Cost Index, which measures civilian earnings.

Thus, a sergeant's base pay and housing allowance rose 20.5 percent between 2001 and 2009, when the average enlisted military member was earning $50,747 in base pay and housing—not including other allowances and bonuses. Officer pay rose 9.1 percent, to an average of $94,700.

The fiscal reality facing us means that we also have to look at the growth in personnel costs which are a major driver of budget growth and are, simply put, on an unsustainable course.

Congress also demanded that the Pentagon absorb a larger share of the housing costs of military families. Their housing allowance was bumped up by 5.7 percent in 2007, another 4.7 percent in 2008 and 5 percent in 2009. Currently, the Pentagon pays all housing costs for families who live off base. Other benefits include shopping at on-base commissaries, which typically save military shoppers about 30 percent on groceries.

Base pay and housing allowance boosts the income of an Army master sergeant with 10 years of service, living at Fort Drum, N.Y., to $84,666.48 a year, according to the current Pentagon pay tables. This sergeant would pay a tax rate of 15 percent, a $6,417.40 tax advantage over civilians.

An Army captain with six years of service with the 10th Mountain Division at Fort Drum, earns $85,330.80 a year in pay and housing allowance—not counting bonuses, tax-free danger pay for service in a war zone and other benefits. A brigadier (one-star) general at Fort Drum, with 16 years of service, is earning $131,652 a year plus a housing allowance of $2,247 per month.

Growth in Personnel Costs Are Unsustainable

"The fiscal reality facing us means that we also have to look at the growth in personnel costs which are a major driver of budget growth and are, simply put, on an unsustainable course," soon-to-retire Defense Secretary Leon Panetta said in

October 2011. Months later, the White House included in its budget proposal a timid increase of between $31 and $128 a month in the health insurance premiums paid by military retirees, unchanged since 1985. That proposal was trashed by Congress.

But in the new era of budget austerity and tough choices, that kind of congressional protection may not last.

"Our folks are worried about whether they're going to get paid, what support services aren't going to be there to help them and their families," said Joyce Raezer, executive director of the National Military Family Association. She defended the increases in pay and benefits by saying, "We've been at war. We've had to pay for people to be at war."

The inevitable cuts in defense spending could, if not managed properly, hurt military families, she said. For instance, whittling down the size of the active duty force could put more of a burden on families if the global missions the military is expected to fill aren't reduced as well. "We are going to be an on-call force, there is going to be trouble somewhere, and if there are fewer people, the ones left will be on call more often," said Raezer, a long-time military spouse.

She also worries that cuts in family support programs will drive reductions in mental health services just at a time when they are most needed.

"We're not saying all these programs will be needed forever," said Raezer. But in all the talk about budget cuts and dwindling resources, she said, there is no thoughtful plan to reduce spending in a rational way.

"What we see coming," she said, "is budget cuts first—and then figuring out how to do with less."

Clarification [by editor of *The Huffington Post* in response to criticism of the article as it first appeared]: *Language has been added to clarify the calculations of base pay and allowance increases for specific members of the military. Original language in the headline and copy referring to "Lavish Benefits" was inac-*

curate and reflected neither the views of David Wood nor The Huffington Post. *We regret the mischaracterization.*

Congressional Report Suggests Pay, Benefit Cuts

Rick Maze

Rick Maze is a staff writer for Navy Times.

A new congressional report says military compensation programs are ripe for budget cuts because the services are having little problem recruiting or retaining qualified service members at a time when personnel costs are soaring.

The report, released Wednesday [November 14, 2012] by the nonpartisan Congressional Budget Office [CBO], comes as no surprise. Congress and the Defense Department [DoD] have wrestled for years over rising personnel costs and the politically difficult decision to change pay and benefits programs, which can be perceived as a reduction in support for current and former service members.

The report, *Costs of Military Pay and Benefits in the Defense Budget,* with its recommendations for ways to cut costs, comes just as President [Barack] Obama and congressional leaders are beginning to engage on what to include in a $1.2 trillion deficit reduction package.

Obama and congressional leaders are meeting Friday [November 16, 2012] to discuss differences. At a Wednesday news conference, Obama said he expected the key sticking point to be what, if any, tax and revenue increases will be included. If that can be resolved, he said it would not take long to work out a compromise on cuts in federal spending. He made no specific mention of cutting defense.

The CBO report says the Defense Department can, for example, control the cost of cash compensation by capping military raises, and by relying more on bonuses and special pays to recruit and retain service members in critical jobs and specialties who might otherwise leave for private-sector employment.

Bigger bonuses in lieu of pay increases . . . save money over time because bonuses do not factor into calculations of military retired pay, the [CBO] report notes.

Defense officials have already said they want to cap raises beginning in 2015 so that basic pay increases for troops are smaller than annual hikes in average private-sector salaries, but CBO says there is room for the military to be even tighter with increases. Defense officials plan to propose a 0.5 percent pay increase in 2015, a 1 percent increase in 2016 and a 1.5 percent increase in 2017, a cumulative savings of $16 billion over 10 years.

Even smaller raises would save more money, the CBO report says.

"Although retention of military personnel might suffer, that effect could be mitigated by boosting the amounts available for selective reenlistment bonuses [SRBs]," the report says. "One advantage of shifting some portion of cash compensation from basic pay to SRBs is that such bonuses are paid only to service members who have come to the end of an obligated term of service and are deciding whether to reenlist. That makes SRBs much more cost-effective than providing a pay raise to the entire force as a way to retain some fraction of the total."

Bigger bonuses in lieu of pay increases also save money over time because bonuses do not factor into calculations of military retired pay, the report notes.

Saving Money in the Retirement System

Defense officials have not made a specific proposal to overhaul military retired pay, but they have asked Congress to approve an independent commission to look at money-saving changes in the retirement system.

The CBO report says radical overhaul is possible by replacing the defined benefit available after 20 years of service with a personal pre-tax retirement benefit based on the federal Thrift Savings Plan.

Even if DoD grandfathers all current service members so they are not affected, such a change could create immediate savings by reducing how much money the services have to put away each year to fund the future retired pay of current service members, the report says.

For 2012, the retirement contribution for future benefits was about $52 billion, the CBO said. The report does not estimate the size of the savings, saying this decision would be made by DoD actuaries who calculate retirement costs.

Health care is another area ripe for savings, the congressional report says. DoD has been trying to sell Congress on various proposals to make beneficiaries shoulder more of the costs of Tricare health coverage, but lawmakers have balked, proposing to cap future increases at no more than the annual cost-of-living adjustment in military retired pay, usually just a few percentage points.

Providing ammunition for those who want to shift more Tricare costs to military retirees and their families, the congressional report says the total Tricare Prime out-of-pocket costs for a military retiree family is just 18 percent of what a nonmilitary family would pay for the same benefit.

The report makes no cost-cutting suggestions beyond those already proposed by DoD and rejected by Congress.

Military Pay: Payroll Is Bloating the Defense Budget, It's Time to Consider Pay Cuts

Mike Cooper

Mike Cooper writes for PolicyMic, an Internet news and opinion site.

An article on Military.com raises the question of whether we overpay members of our military. As a vet, you'd probably assume that I'm dead set against cutting military pay. You'd be wrong.

Payroll is, like in most organizations, a huge chunk of the military's annual budget. According to militarypaychart.us, the Army's payroll for 2012 was $44.205 billion. That's officer and enlisted pay combined. For 2013, the Army's projected budget is $43.925 billion, a slight overall reduction. Here's the thing, officer pay for 2013 is projected to *increase* very slightly, leaving the enlisted fighters to take up the entire payroll reduction and then some.

This doesn't mean enlisted folks will get paid any less as individuals. What it means is that there will be fewer enlisted folks. Most of the officers will stick around and continue to enjoy longevity pay increases. Wait a minute, you should be saying to yourself (if not out loud), don't the enlisted guys do all the actual work? Why yes, yes they do. I'm not suggesting that the military doesn't need officers, but if you're going to cut back on the force, I'd suggest cutting back on overhead, not production.

This is why it's essential that the military look at cutting pay. You can't keep the same number of enlisted soldiers and sailors on duty and cut the payroll at the same time. Something has to give. Cutting the number of officers would be a good start, but you've got to have *some* leadership; you can't eliminate the entire officer corps. Which means you've got to consider other options.

A single E4 in the Army has virtually no expenses. This is why barracks parking lots are jammed full of stylish new cars.

As clearly sympathetic to enlisted folks as I am, you may be wondering how I could possibly consider cutting their pay. Well, here's the deal. They get paid better than many of you. The Army uses this fact as a recruiting tool (see an example here).

A corporal in the Army (E-4, a junior rank to which virtually every single enlisted solider rises within 2 years) earns $27,200 in base pay after 4 years of service. That's not a lot of money, but consider that *the Army also provides housing and food*, work clothes (more on that shortly), *and* health care. So, a single E4 in the Army has virtually no expenses. This is why barracks parking lots are jammed full of stylish new cars and also why the streets leading into any major military installation are lined with dealers of both new and used cars. Also tattoo parlors and strip clubs. And pawn shops. (Young enlisted troops are notoriously bad money managers, so pawn shops and pay day lenders are two of the five pillars of commerce in any military town.)

Many soldiers are eligible for on-post/on-base housing too, although the Army at least is leaning toward contracting out family quarters, so it's now treated pretty much like off-post housing. In other words, the Army gives you an allowance for rent and you pay your landlord with the money. For an E4, regardless of time served, that housing allowance is about $14,000 per year but varies on location. It can be much higher but is unlikely to be much lower. The basic monthly rates differ depending on your marital status: $588 for single soldiers who choose not to live in barracks and $784 for married soldiers, with or without kids. Is that enough to rent a house or apartment? Nope. But, does your employer give you money for rent on top of your monthly pay? Mine doesn't.

All told, an E4 brings in around $50k per year. Making E4 requires no college education and no advanced military training beyond basic and initial job training, which is often cursory at best.

One very unique allowance is called "BAH Diff." It's a differential housing allowance for formerly married soldiers with child support obligations. In other words, the Army basically pays child support for many divorced soldiers. This probably amounts to a nice chunk of the budget because the military is tough on marriages. I have long believed that military service should be limited to unmarried individuals not because we're paying too much child support for divorced soldiers but because, even in peacetime, the miltary is simply no place to raise a family. (I'm perfectly happy to discuss this separately and may get around to writing about it later.)

There is a raft of other incentive pay, to include combat pay, jump pay, and flight pay. There's also an annual clothing allowance; for an E4 with 4 years in service this amounts to over $440 per year. Subsistence allowance (meals) for enlisted personnel is currently $348 per month.

All told, an E4 brings in around $50k per year. Making E4 requires no college education and no advanced military training beyond basic and initial job training, which is often cursory at best.

I'm not knocking enlisted ranks, but facts are facts. You don't have to be a highly trained fighting machine to be an E4. You've just got to have a super-human ability to deal with bullshit, marginally qualified superiors, and some physical discomfort. In other words, it's very much like many civilian jobs except that you cannot just walk in one day and tell the boss to shove it.

Getting shot at is a risk but only if you're deployed. The civilian job pay comparison above compares the pay of a civilian cop and a military cop. I'm no big fan of cops, but many, if not most, civilian cops risk life and limb every day in their own home towns. It's worth asking which deserves better pay. Of course this depends largely on your opinion of U.S. military intervention overseas (which also costs a LOT of money and is sometimes truly worth it).

There's another area where the military could save a few million without affecting readiness one iota: uniforms.

I've long argued that the Army wastes hundreds of thousands of dollars every year on dress uniforms. Every single enlistee gets one upon graduation and every one of these uniforms costs the Army approximately $300.00. Most soldiers will never wear this uniform for anything other than monthly inspections. I wore my dress uniform once and only once in four years. Dress uniforms should be issued on an as needed basis; most enlisted soldiers will never need one.

The Army has also spent billions of dollars *changing* uniforms. The current green dress uniform is now being phased out in favor of a new dress blue. The Advanced Combat Uniform (ACU) is also being phased out after a mere 8 years because it doesn't work. The Physical Training (PT) uniform has been changed at least a few times in recent years. Last year, the beret was dumped as the standard headgear in favor of the patrol cap which it replaced just 10 years ago (a stupid and divisive move—the beret is an utterly useless piece of headgear which looks awful when worn incorrectly, as it often is). Each time the Army changes uniforms, billions of dollars are involved and the change is not always for the better.

Comparisons of Military and Civilian Pay Overlook Hidden Expenses of Military Families

Sarah Smiley

Sarah Smiley is an author and syndicated columnist whose writing appears in publications across the country.

A January [2013] article [the first viewpoint in this chapter] by David Wood for the *Huffington Post* has risen from the dead, and it's making many military families mad—again.

The article, "Defense Budget Faces Cuts to Personnel After Decade of War," has more than 60 pages of comments, half of which were made within days of its release on January 30. On page 31, however, after nearly a month of silence, the comments picked up again on March 11. Soon after, it went viral in the military community.

I don't know who dug up this relatively old column, but according to an editor's note at the bottom, "language has been added [post-publication] to clarify" some calculations, making this piece of walking-dead commentary something like Frankenstein. It's been patched up and given new life, and now it's terrorizing the military community.

Oh, and the "monster" is still evolving.

Under pressure and scrutiny, Wood has revised his text multiple times. His original opening sentence was probably the scariest of all—"For more than a decade, Congress and the Pentagon have lavished money on the nation's 1.3 million active-duty troops and their families"—but the word "lavished" has since been deleted.

Semantics and edit-and-rewrite-as-you-go journalism aside, Wood's biggest problem is his apples-to-apples approach to military versus civilian pay that overlooks the hidden costs of military life.

"Since 2001, total military compensation . . . grew by 20.5 percent, while comparable private-sector civilian pay did not increase at all," Wood writes. "The cost of military compensation rose steeply even though the size of the active-duty force grew by only 3 percent during that period."

We military families don't understand Wood's confusion with this. The pay grew by 20.5 percent because of everything that the slightly increased force has been expected to do since 2001—mainly, more frequent and longer deployments.

To make his point about military and civilian pay, Wood states that an Army master sergeant who has been in the service since 9/11 [2001] and is stationed at Fort Drum makes about $85,000 a year. This number is deceiving. Also, it's highly unlikely that anyone would rise to the rank of master sergeant in 10 years. Even so, the base pay for a master sergeant with 10 years of service is about $50,000 a year. Allowances for housing and cost of living would be added to the base pay according to the location of the duty station.

But let's go with Wood's figure anyway.

Our "free health care" equates to being seen at government-run hospitals that are equivalent in inefficiency and frustration to the Department of Motor Vehicles.

Invalid Comparisons

According to the U.S. Department of Labor's website CareerOneStop, an accountant in 2011 could expect to make about $109,900 in a year.

But the accountant is coming home every night. He doesn't leave his family for a year at a time (which often increases child care expenses). And, in general, he doesn't move every three years (more on this below). His life isn't at the whim of the U.S. government. He can wear what he chooses, take vacation when he prefers, and besides a boss and his customers, he doesn't answer to anyone.

Yes, the accountant probably has to pay for health care, and he doesn't get tax-free groceries, but, well, he's making $20,000 more than the guy who's risking his life overseas.

All of the above is why Wood's whining about military shoppers' 30 percent savings on groceries at the commissary falls on unsympathetic ears. Yes, we have access to tax-free groceries, but my husband is required to buy, out of his own pay, many of his uniforms—the same ones the military forces him to wear. We don't get a company car. And our "free health care" equates to being seen at government-run hospitals that are equivalent in inefficiency and frustration to the Department of Motor Vehicles.

Wood leaves these comparisons out, focusing only on what military families get on paper. But even those facts don't always add up.

> To say that service members have an overabundance of allowances and bonuses is inaccurate and frankly offensive.

Wood writes, "[T]he Pentagon pays all housing costs for families who live off base." This is absolutely false. The military gives us a housing allowance based on local civilian housing markets. And it's not the "lavish" market, either.

That same hypothetical master sergeant making $50,000 in base pay would get an additional $2,300 monthly for housing if he was stationed in Washington, D.C. The average rate for a 2-bedroom apartment near D.C. is $2,341.

But these figures say nothing to the fact that military families can rarely build equity in a home. In 13 years of marriage, [husband] Dustin and I have moved a half-dozen times, and we've lost money in real estate every single time.

I agree with Wood that there are many areas of wasted spending in the military. As with any government agency, it is full of redundancies, inefficiencies and frustrations. The general public will learn more about this when they, too, are in government-run health care. But to say that service members have an overabundance of allowances and bonuses is inaccurate and frankly offensive.

While Wood is hurriedly deleting his words and "facts," making edits as the pressure ensues, may I suggest that he go ahead and backspace over the whole thing, sending this Frankenstein back to the lab?

Claims That Service Members Are Overpaid Ignore the Sacrifices They and Their Families Make

Tony Carr

Tony Carr is a retired Air Force officer, veteran advocate, and blogger. He is a former combat pilot and squadron commander.

David Wood [journalist] enjoys something most members of the US military do not. He has the luxury of performing poorly in his job and living to tell about it.

Mr. Wood published a *Huffington Post* article [the first viewpoint in this chapter] earlier this year [January 2013] originally titled "After a Decade of Lavish Benefits, Military Personnel Fear Cuts." This lamentable array of words, a cheap literary hook designed to ensnare fiscally paranoid readers by construing military members as trough-feeding elites defensively crouched over burgeoning piles of cash, was inexplicably changed Tuesday [March 13, 2013]. But not before Mr. Wood managed to rack up nearly 40,000 votes of approval on Facebook. And not before he managed to cultivate an ugly and undeserved myth that can only harm the soul of a nation: the myth that America's fighting men and women are some sort of high-on-the-hog mercenary force. Nothing could be further from the truth.

Mr. Wood, though you're likely to never read these words, let me address you directly as a veteran. I understand that you're against war in general. I understand you were against the invasion of Iraq. It might surprise you just how many veterans agree with you on these matters. But sir, despite your admirable credentials and even given the benefit of the doubt, you've managed to pen an article so careless with the image of the American veteran that it should not have seen the light of day. I assume without meaning to do so, you've insulted the quiet, unassuming ethic of the American veteran by saying things that beg to be challenged, thereby inviting your subjects to defend themselves against your words, which they do at the risk of appearing prideful, something almost universally abhorred in the veteran culture.

So I appeal to you, Mr. Wood. Before you pick up your pen again, take care in your thoughts and how you express them. Take care that you don't express manifestly incorrect notions that your readership, trusting your Pulitzer [Prize-winning] credentials and your evident sensibility, might wrongly share, forward, and ultimately, legitimize.

The real question is whether a country manifestly out of touch with the true costs of the foreign activism it serially endorses is deserving of [military people's] selflessness.

Claims That Military Pay Is Excessive Are Not True

To say that military pay and benefits have "soared far above civilian comparison" is either misguided or disingenuous, but in either case, deeply wrong. To the extent military pay and benefits have been kept competitive, this has been necessary to keep enough qualified warriors in uniform to get the job done. If anything, the use of pay has been a cynical installment employed to prevent mass abandonment of an activity bent on grinding people and their families into a fine powder. The level of sacrifice asked of our military in recent years is historically unprecedented, and America's warriors are not getting rich enduring it. In fact, 1.5 million of them need food stamps to supplement their incomes, scores have trouble finding post-service employment, and tens of thousands will live the rest of their lives without ever being made whole again, having left things on the battlefield that defy monetary valuation. Military members make their decisions concerning whether or not to stay in uniform on the basis of many criteria, pay and benefits among these. Each family has its own situation and hence its own calculus. *C'est la guerre* ["that's war"]. But until machine press operators and gas station attendants start spending 12 months away from their families and living constantly under the threat of getting blown apart by an IED [improvised explosive device], you and your readers should consider any comparison of military and civilian pay fundamentally invalid.

> *You have your cross-hairs on the wrong target. Aim at the bureaucracies unable to effectively manage the resources generously provided by the American people and you'll have something closer to a valid critique.*

But just out of curiosity . . . who exactly do you think is overpaid? Generalities are fun, but whose "lavish" pay should be slashed? The 20-year-old Ohioan struggling to understand Pashto [Iranian language] while he orchestrates installation of a water filtration system in a village that has resisted improvement since before Alexander the Great? Maybe the 32-year-old Californian responsible for guiding a 50,000-pound aircraft moving at the speed of sound to a precise point in time and space where she will deliver a Volkswagen-sized munition to a point on the Earth no bigger than a hopscotch court . . . knowing she will kill her own teammates or allow the enemy to kill them if she gets it wrong? Or maybe the 40-year-old Floridian whose success is defined by whether his ability to train, motivate, inspire, and focus the 500 people in his charge will be enough to keep them alive in a war where neither the enemy nor the objective are understood and the source of the next attack is never known? You're not talking about "personnel" my friend . . . you're talking about "people." Individuals with talents, capabilities, and courage that scare the living hell out of enemies. They are a bargain at twice the current rate, fiscal pressures be damned.

But while we're on the point. People don't make Master Sergeant in the Army in 10 years and they certainly don't make Brigadier General in 16 years. But if they did, why would the pay you decry be so unreasonable? We're talking about educated, capable, fit, ingenious men and women capable of taking life one minute, saving it the next, then opening a homeless shelter before sundown. They work tirelessly and sleep optionally. I've been known to bash a general or two in my time, but the vast majority of them could step into any boardroom in America and, before the first coffee mug hit the table, instantly distill the winners and losers in the room, mentally devise a strategy for the next six months of corporate operations, and spend the next hour memorizing the names of the children and pets of everyone in the room. These people you construe as fat cats are not "ordinary people doing extraordinary things" as the old trope goes. They are extraordinary people making amazing things look easy. The real question is whether a country manifestly out of touch with the true costs of the foreign activism it serially endorses is deserving of their selflessness.

Military Families Receive Too Little

What is not in question is that their families deserve Sainthood. Your assertions that day care and counseling services are overfunded would be laughable if the entire subject matter weren't already submerged in an ocean of tears that's been swelling for a dozen years. Disabuse yourself of the notion that parents enjoy spending a year or more without their counterparts, forced to leave their children with strangers if they dare seek a trip to the movie theater. And when these patient and brave spouses who have selflessly given away a normal relationship with their mate in the name of Afghan or Iraqi freedom sense themselves approaching the rocky shoals of sanity, they need only dial an 800 number to receive some of that Cadillac counseling you wrote about. Many of the things you see as overfunded enhancements are actually viewed as running jokes within the military. The kind told by sad comics. In other words, you have your cross-hairs on the wrong target. Aim at the bureaucracies unable to effectively manage the resources generously provided by the American people and you'll have something closer to a valid critique. Aim at the politicians who flung us into undeclared and under-resourced wars, and you'll have the root cause dead to rights.

There's plenty of room for reform in national defense. Operations are not immune to waste, and anecdotally, there are unnecessary deployments still taking place in our war effort. With a price tag of one million dollars per warrior per year deployed, this is the real story for reform-minded journalists looking to cast a light on costly inefficiencies. You ask or imply valid questions about whether commissaries and exchanges should be reformed, and it's fair to ask retirees like me to pay a little more for health care. In fact, I agree with the seed of your column, which seems to hold that undue deference to the military is inappropriate, and can actually poison the civil-military discourse we depend upon to ensure the lives of our men and women are not cheaply risked. A bit more journalistic bravado in challenging military leaders a decade ago, for example, might have disrupted the march to war in Iraq, a debacle directly responsible for nearly all of the consequences your article bemoans. But all these points aside, your article was far more wrong than right.

When military people are wrong, their teammates die. Airplanes hit mountains. Artillery shells fall on civilians. Incorrect targets are bombed. Ships run aground. Military servants are unable to comprehend consequence-free failure, which is why some are mystified that the tone and substance of your article continue uncorrected. Whatever your intent, you were wrong, Mr. Wood. In the immortal words of Colonel Nathan R. Jessup, "you have that luxury." And I know many who will continue making certain you and I and others have that luxury . . . by laying their lives on the line.

Financial Struggles Are Common Among Military Families

Donna Gordon Blankinship

Donna Gordon Blankinship is a staff writer for the Associated Press.

Military families aren't surprised when they hear about the financial struggles that Staff Sgt. Robert Bales, his wife and children faced at home. It's part of their lives, too.

They say money problems can never justify doing what the military says Bales did: kill 17 civilians in a nighttime shooting rampage through two Afghan villages on March 11 [2012]. Still, the details emerging about his life served as a prominent reminder of the hardship they have endured over a decade of two wars.

"The stress factors with the families is just unbelievable," said Roger J. Mealey, a Vietnam veteran who runs a website to aid struggling military families.

While laws give active-duty soldiers extra combat pay, provide housing allowances and exempt them from taxes, experts say, families are straining under multiple deployments, frequent relocations and the difficulty spouses have in getting and keeping jobs in new cities.

A 2010 military survey found that 27 percent of service members said they had more than $10,000 in credit card debt, while 16 percent of civilians do. The study also found more than a third of military families have trouble paying monthly bills, and more than 20 percent reported borrowing money outside of banks.

Service members and their families do have access to financial counselors, but many shy away from it because they don't want their commanders to know, said Andi Wrenn, a financial and relationship counselor in Boston [Massachusetts] who has worked with service members.

The unemployment rate among military spouses is about 26 percent, according to a report from the nonprofit group, Iraq and Afghanistan Veterans of America.

Bales' life reflected some of that financial turmoil.

Court records and interviews showed that he joined the military 11 years ago after a Florida investment went sour. He had a Seattle [Washington]-area home condemned, struggled to make payments on another and failed to get a promotion a year ago. His wife has had two, one-year jobs since leaving Washington Mutual four years ago.

His wife put up their Lake Tapps, Wash., home for sale days before the rampage. They bought the home in 2005, records show, for $280,000. They listed it for $229,000.

Many of the organizations are just giving handouts and not trying to fix the underlying financial problems the troops face.

Nonprofits Help Military Families

Last year, Mealey connected nearly 300 military families just like the Bales family with another 300 "angels" willing to help them pay a few bills or send a gift card. He said he answers calls and emails every week from military families who are having problems negotiating base life.

Their pleas for help are posted on a simple red-white-and-blue website: a soldier at Fort Stewart, Ga., with a wife and two kids can't afford $300 for a new dress uniform; a veteran in St. Louis [Missouri] with a wife and two kids needs help with power bills; and a San Diego [California] Navy wife with four kids just got laid off from her job.

Mealey's website is one of more than 40,000 nonprofits, big and small, trying to help the troops these days. They're called the "sea of goodwill," said Kate Kohler, a [United States Military Academy at] West Point graduate and Army captain who is the chief operating officer of the PenFed Foundation, a nonprofit that helps troops with financial literacy, housing and emergency needs.

She said their hearts are in the right place but so many of the organizations are just giving handouts and not trying to fix the underlying financial problems the troops face.

It's not easy supporting four people on a staff sergeant's salary—about $39,000 a year—especially when one member of the family keeps getting sent overseas.

Although Kohler's organization also gives emergency loans and grants, most come with some required financial literacy training.

The mostly young service members have little experience dealing with their own finances and don't know what to do with the ups and downs of military life. She described one symptom as the Disneyland effect: overspending when troops return home to make up for lost time with family.

An Iraq War vet who runs an organization to help veterans and active-duty military said he sympathized with Bales' family and other military families.

It's not easy supporting four people on a staff sergeant's salary—about $39,000 a year—especially when one member of the family keeps getting sent overseas, said Patrick Bellon, executive director of Veterans for Common Sense.

Laws Protecting Military Families Are Not Enforced

There are laws to protect military families from speedy foreclosures and predatory lenders, but Bellon wasn't confident those laws are being enforced.

Mortgage lenders and landlords are supposed to give military families more time to make their payments during a deployment. The armed forces have several employment programs to help military spouses, including special training for jobs they can take with them from base to base.

"It just frustrates me," said Mealey, who started his one-man New Beginnings website for military families in 2003 after retiring from Motorola.

After the wars in Iraq and Afghanistan started, he wanted to find a way to help the troops.

"If we're asking them to serve their country and put their life on the line, I don't think their families should be put in the position where they're sleeping on the floor or don't have enough food to feed their kids," Mealey said.

Food Stamp Use at Military Commissaries up Sharply in Four Years

Seth Robbins

Seth Robbins is a reporter for the military newspaper Stars and Stripes. *He is based in Baumholder, Germany.*

Food stamp purchases at military commissaries have nearly tripled during the last four years, according to Defense Commissary Agency figures.

The agency reports that nearly $88 million worth of food stamps were used at commissaries nationwide in 2011, up from $31 million in 2008.

There is little information about who is using the food stamps, officially called the Supplemental Nutrition Assistance Program by the Department of Agriculture, because DeCA and the Defense Department do not keep data on individuals who purchase items at commissaries. But Joyce Raezer, the executive director of the National Military Family Association, suspects that the majority of food stamp users are veterans who separated before retirement and members of the National Guard or reserve forces.

"I suspect that we are talking about more recently [separated]," she said, "who have gotten out of the military and found out that it's not easy to find a job in the civilian sector."

Nearly 860,000 veterans filed for unemployment benefits last month, of whom more than one-quarter are young veterans, according to Bureau of Labor Statistics.

Raezer said she has also heard that members of the reserve forces and the National Guard are increasingly seeking help from organizations that provide emergency assistance to military families.

"I would be willing to suspect they have been demobilized, they are off active duty, but their civilian job isn't there anymore," she said.

Raezer, who has been following the issue of food stamp usage at commissaries for more than a decade, said that very few active-duty servicemembers qualify for food stamps "because military pay has improved so much" over the last decade.

A 2003 Department of Defense study, the most recent available, found that 2,100 active-duty members received food stamps in 2002. The number was much lower than the 19,400 receiving food stamps in 1991.

The military ... started its own food assistance program, the Family Subsistence Supplemental Allowance, or FSSA, in 2001 to remove military families from the food stamp program.

"We are working with the Department of Agriculture on an updated study now," said DOD spokeswoman Eileen M. Lainez in an email.

The 2003 study showed that the majority of active-duty servicemembers who qualified for food stamp assistance lived in base housing. Housing is not calculated as part of servicemembers' income, and many would not have qualified for the program had the cost of housing been included, the study found.

"The fact that some enlisted members and even a few officers received (food stamps) was more a result of larger household sizes and live-in government quarters than an indicator of inadequate military compensation," said Lainez.

The military, however, started its own food assistance program, the Family Subsistence Supplemental Allowance, or FSSA, in 2001 to remove military families from the food stamp program.

The program provides servicemembers with families up to $1,100 monthly, depending on household income and family size. All servicemembers can apply, but the majority who receive the allowance are junior enlisted servicemembers who enter the military with large families, said Lainez.

In 2010, 510 servicemembers qualified for the program, receiving more than $1.3 million in aid. That figure was a jump from 2009, when 245 servicemembers qualified for the program and received about $737,000.

Still, it's a tiny group, considering that there are now more than 1.4 million servicemembers, Lainez said: "This represents .000375 (.0375%) or less than four-one hundredths of one percent of the active duty population."

The steep economic downturn began in the fall of 2008, and the sharpest year-to-year growth in food stamp usage at commissaries was from 2008 to 2009, increasing nearly 70 percent to $53 million.

Bases overseas do not accept food stamps.

During this time, civilian use of food stamps also increased significantly, from about $35 billion to more than $50 billion. In 2010, the Dept. of Agriculture reported there were $65 billion worth of food stamp purchases nationwide.

The commissaries sell items at cost, with a 5 percent surcharge. According to the DeCA website, this model saves patrons an average of 30 percent when contrasted with commercial prices.

John Smith, a spokesman for Operation Homefront, a non-profit organization that provides emergency assistance to military families, said his organization has seen the amount of food assistance it provides to military families double since 2008.

The nature of military service, in which servicemembers are constantly moving to new assignments, often has unintended consequences on the income of military families, he said.

"All of a sudden your spouse can't work anymore," he said. "And there is a potential crisis right there."

What Personal and Social Problems Do Military Families Face?

Chapter Preface

The unique problems of military families are unfamiliar to most other citizens. Chief among them are the difficulties imposed by repeated PCS (Permanent Change of Station) moves. In the first place, moving is hard work. The military pays for professional packing and moving of household goods, up to an amount depending on rank of the service member and size of the family. But organizing personal belongings, discarding those that can't be taken, and unpacking at the destination is frustrating, especially if new living quarters are not found right away. There is often a long waiting list for on-base housing; people who cannot obtain it, or who prefer to live off base, must devote time and effort to house-hunting and may perhaps even stay temporarily in a motel. On top of this there is a lot of paperwork, such as transferring school and medical records; obtaining new driver's licenses; and for overseas moves, getting passports, visas, and medical screenings.

A problem that sometimes arises in moving is that in certain cases the family must give up a pet. Some military bases limit the number of pets per household or will not allow certain breeds of dogs. In the case of off-base housing, it may be impossible to find rentals that will accept any pets at all. There are organizations that help arrange foster care for the pets that service members are temporarily unable to keep, but even when this proves possible, separation from a beloved pet is sad.

The most serious potential result of a PCS is the hardship a military family faces if the service member's spouse cannot find a new job, or must take a job that does not utilize his or her training and ability. As of 2011, the unemployment rate of military spouses was 26 percent, more than three times the national average, and the actual jobless rate was higher counting military spouses who were not actively seeking a job but would have liked to have one. Despite a number of programs to help them, such as the Joining Forces project launched by First Lady Michelle Obama and "Second Lady" Jill Biden (the wife of Vice President Joe Biden), there are still far too many out of work. The problem is partly that it is difficult for people with occupations requiring state certification or licensing to get certified in a new state. Also, military spouses' employment histories generally show numerous job changes and frequent breaks, which suggests to employers that the person may not be able to stay long enough to justify on-the-job training. And in some fields, there simply may not be any local job openings.

In the April 2013 issue of *Fortune* magazine, Mrs. Obama and Mrs. Biden wrote, "This is an all-hands-on-deck issue, and we cannot rest until every single veteran and military spouse who is searching for a job has found one. These men and women have sacrificed so much for all of us. Now is the time for all of us to come together to serve them as well as they have served this country."

For same-sex military spouses there are special problems. Until early 2013, they were not entitled to any of the benefits other military families receive. Since that time, those in permanent, committed relationships have had the right to such things as military ID cards; commissary privileges; morale, welfare, and recreational programs; child care; membership in Family Readiness Groups; casualty notification; hospital visitation privileges; joint assignments for dual-military couples; and more. But there were still many rights and financial benefits that they did not have because under the federal Defense of Marriage Act (DOMA) they could not legally be given them, even if they were married in states that legalized same-sex marriage. In June 2013, the US Supreme Court ruled that DOMA was unconstitutional, so the rules regarding specific benefits will soon be changed. The situation is complicated by the frequency of military moves, since same-sex couples may no longer live in a state that recognizes their marriage, or may never have lived in a state that allows it; they are now being granted short leaves for travel to a state where they can get married.

"We owe every member of our armed forces a tremendous debt for their service, sacrifice, and bravery," said US Representative Colleen Hanabusa, a cosponsor of the Military Spouses Equal Treatment Act. "Our commitment to honoring them as outstanding Americans must include recognizing their spouses and families—regardless of sexual orientation."

The Emotional Well-being of Military Families Depends on Their Members' Mutual Support

Ellen Weber Libby

Ellen Weber Libby is a clinical psychologist with a private psychotherapy practice in Washington, DC. She is the author of The Favorite Child, *published in 2010.*

In this time of national political and social discord, one belief shared by many Americans is that men and women serving in the military, as well as their families, make enormous personal sacrifices. Americans have general notions of the hardships endured by personnel deployed to war zones: being separated from families; living in Spartan conditions and without the familiar comforts of home; patrolling in dangerous and stressful conditions; coping with difficult emotions generated by deaths and injuries to comrades.

The images of the hardships endured by their families are usually more vague. The family system, like any other system either adapts or falls apart when a vital part of the system, like a spouse or parent, is absent for a prolonged period of time. Generally, military families do not fall apart when a member is deployed. They adapt with the assistance of officers' wives, formal and informal military support systems, extended families, and the broader community. The family's success at coping often reflects the emotional strength of the parent left stateside and the preexisting mental health of the family, i.e., how successfully the family contributes to the emotional well-being of each member.

Parents left stateside develop their own ways of operating as they are forced to take on responsibilities that were previously shared. Some spouses enthusiastically take on the challenges while others do so with resentment. As the family adapts to daily life without one parent, children may become more independent because the at-home parent has less time and has to be more discriminating about tending to their children's need. Older children may grow to fill voids created by their absent parent and younger children may become more reliant on older siblings. While the family system adapts, each member usually matures through developing an array of required functional, interpersonal, and psychological skills. Growing confidence and a sense of personal power often accompanies this progression.

Families functioning with one involved parent and one absent parent are particularly vulnerable to the adverse affects of the favorite child complex.

Army Wives, the hit *Lifetime* show that is avidly followed by many military spouses, poignantly dramatizes the stresses added to ordinary family life by the demands of being married to someone who serves in the military, especially during times of war. Some military wives comment on the show's website that finally, they feel seen and appreciated. The show illustrates a phenomenon that I have observed among military families with whom I have worked—that re-integrating the family after deployment is often more stressful than adapting to the deployment itself.

The Danger of Favoring One Child

Further, military families are particularly vulnerable to the negative repercussions of the favorite child complex. In the book, *The Favorite Child*, I describe the impact on families when a given parent favors a given child because that child fills needs of that parent. Parents left stateside have many varied needs left unmet when their partners are deployed. These parents are susceptible to favoring the child who instinctively meets their needs, whether they do chores around the house without being asked or offer social companionship at the end of a long day.

In exchange for filling their parent's needs, these children are rewarded, often with inappropriate privileges and by not being held accountable for their behaviors. Left unattended, these favorite children can grow up vulnerable to feelings of entitlement and to believing that rules do not apply to them. The entire family is impacted, often adversely, by the coupling of the given parent and child. Families functioning with one involved parent and one absent parent are particularly vulnerable to the adverse affects of the favorite child complex. In military families coping with the deployment of one adult, the absence of one parent is real, not just a psychological dynamic making the family more susceptible to the negative consequences of this complex.

When the deployed parent returns, again the family system must readjust. Often this reintegration is more challenging than was the original separation and is more difficult to work through than expected. Soldiers, in their absences, had experiences profoundly influencing their personalities. Most often they return very different than the people who left. And, in their absences, life moved on for their families. By necessity, family members had to adapt to life without them.

How relationships integrate these disparate experiences impacts the ultimate mental health of all family members.

- Returning soldiers are different people, their personalities affected by battlefield experiences.

- Stateside parents are different people, their personalities affected by the added responsibilities they carried during their partners' absences.

- Children are different people, their personalities affected by having coped with the absence of one parent and responded to the requirements of the other parent.

New Relationships Within the Family

The relationships that family members have when they reintegrate after deployment are different than the ones they had at the time of "good bye."

- If a stateside parent and child developed a favored relationship, what happens? Does the child maintain the favored status or is the child relegated back to the status held prior to deployment? Does the child feel rejected or relieved? How does this impact the relationship between this child and the returning parent, and the relationship between the returning parent and other children?

- Stateside parents learned to operate alone. What happens now? Do they readily make room for their partner; or do they feel entitled to "time off," resentful at having been the responsible parent 24/7? Do they resent their returning partner's input, perceiving it as critical, or are they appreciative, perceiving it as supportive?

- Returning partners were not a part of their families' daily lives. How do they fit in? How do they get caught up on the history and experiences they missed? Are family members eager to bringing them up to speed or resentful?

- Returning partners are expected to respond to the demands of daily family life. How do they make the transition from the war zone? Are they respectful of the demands, or in comparison with those experienced when deployed, do they trivialize them?

- Children learned how to function with just one parent. How do the children adjust to the presence of two authority figures? What happens to the responsibilities they fulfilled and privileges they received? Are they eager to reconnect with their parent or angry with them for having been gone?

- Children's ages and the length of parents' deployments impacts the coming together. Do younger children remember the deployed parent, or when they return, are they like strangers? Have older children moved on and developed an independence they cherish, or upon their parent's return, do they demonstrate infantile behaviors in their hunger to be taken care of?

Separations and reunions are a way of life for military families. Adapting to them leads to stress and affects the dynamics of the family. The mental health of all members— parents and children alike—is impacted by the family's skill in addressing the issues posed by these experiences.

Military Pet Policies Tear Families Apart

Alisa Johnson and Theresa Donnelly

Alisa Johnson is the president of Dogs on Deployment, which she and her husband—both military officers—founded to help military members find families and individuals who are willing to foster their pets while they are deployed. Theresa Donnelly is the owner of Hawaii Military Pets, a resource that advocates for standardized pet policies within the Department of Defense.

Many of our country's armed forces willingly lay down their lives, protecting others with their call to honor, to protect and defend our freedom and democracy. According to the White House, there are more than two million men and women who have served in war zones and an unprecedented number of deployments by our National Guardsmen and reservists. The courage of these fine individuals and their families must never be forgotten.

For the overwhelming majority of troops, this family includes their cherished pets. For military families that face constant deployments and other uncertainties, there's comfort knowing a pet will be there to give unconditional love when they return. Videos on the Internet document these emotional reunions filled with wagging tails, uncontrollable licking and animals bouncing around, so excited they can barely walk. Some pets jump right into the arms of their thrilled owners.

Not only do pets help heal the troops, these furry family members help military spouses tremendously as they settle into a home routine without their loved one. Often spouses find themselves doing tasks they would normally have help with, such as raising children alone and sometimes doing so without the support network of close family and friends.

"Nothing can truly fill the hole in my heart when my husband is gone," said Brianda Gracia, a Marine spouse stationed at Marine Corps Base Hawaii. "We have no kids, and my dogs bring me so much love and joy. They make me smile. I would be beyond depressed without my pups."

Considering how vital pets are for stability and love, it's shocking to know there are official military housing pet policies in place, forcing families to abandon cherished pets. This is because there's no standardized pet policy to facilitate forever ownership. Instead, we have inconsistent weight, size and numeric limits. Furthermore, our housing policies include unscientific and unenforceable breed bans.

Inconsistencies in Military Housing

Below are just some examples of the inconsistencies in military housing, and there are many others.

It's not just the bans [on pets], it's numerical limits that are breaking apart families.

Lincoln Military Housing, which owns base housing at Marine Corps bases Camp Lejeune, Camp Pendleton, Twenty-nine Palms and Quantico, as well as large Naval bases NAS Fallon, Lemoore and Norfolk states as their pet policy, "Only two pets, dogs and/or cats are allowed in the home. Full or mixed breeds of pit bulls, Rottweilers, canine/wolf hybrids, or any canine breed with dominant traits of aggression are not permitted aboard the installation or in housing."

Balfour Beatty, a larger company in military privatized base housing, bans not only full or mixed breeds of pit bulls, Rottweilers and canine/wolf hybrids, but also Akitas, Chows, Dobermans, American Staffordshire Terriers and English Staffordshire Bull Terriers. This includes a grandfather clause in their policy that states, "For residents in housing on or before March 31, 2008 these animals will be 'grandfathered' if the resident had this type of pet and it was documented in their housing file. These pets must be muzzled when they are outside of the home."

However, military families have told us that it is often difficult to get a pet grandfathered in, and it only applies to a singular base where the pet was originally owned. In other words, the grandfather clause does not follow the pet, only the base.

And it's not just the bans, it's numerical limits that are breaking apart families. Pinnacle Military Housing allows up to four walking pets, while most base housing allows only two. We have been contacted by several families that lived in housing where they were allowed to keep their two dogs and two cats, but then moved to a housing complex that only allows up to two, forcing them to re-home two of their four pets. Some base housing, including Balfour Beatty, consider a bird cage or fish tank to count as one pet, bringing the total number allowed to one walking pet.

Based on these differing policies of many of the base housing key players, the problem is obvious. There is no consistency and no protection granted to pet owners.

This is the first of a series of blogs to explain why and how this destructive policy is having devastating consequences as military families are forced to give up their family members. We hope by sharing their heartbreaking stories, you'll be inspired to join us in our quest to ask the United States Department of Defense for an overarching pet policy that focuses on education and enforcement, regardless of subjective breed identification.

Out—But Not In: Military Club Closes Ranks to Gay Wife

Ashley Fantz

Ashley Fantz is a reporter for CNN.

For 15 years, Ashley Broadway has devoted her life to the military and to her spouse, an Army lieutenant colonel.

The former schoolteacher found a new job and made new friends each time she had to relocate bases, including a move to South Korea. When a deployment to the Middle East separated the couple, Broadway took care of the couple's young son, Carson, on her own.

Now at Fort Bragg, North Carolina, and with a second child on the way, Broadway wanted to settle down and get to know more spouses like herself.

So she applied for membership to the Association of Bragg Officers' Spouses.

"I thought, 'Here's a chance to make some close friends who would really understand me,'" Broadway said. "And I could get very active in events that help other families like mine. I was excited, really excited, to be a part of this group."

But the Bragg spouse club apparently didn't feel the same way. Broadway's married to Lt. Col. Heather Mack. The officers' spouse club didn't want her, she believes, because she's gay.

Shortly after Broadway applied, the club called her to say it had new membership rules. If she didn't have a military ID card, she couldn't join.

The couple is legally married—reciting their vows during a November ceremony in Washington, D.C., and signing a state marriage certificate.

Though gay people can now serve openly, the military doesn't formally recognize same-sex marriage under the federal Defense of Marriage Act.

Broadway's experience may reflect a struggle at the nation's military bases to adapt culturally to the legal changes brought on by 2011's repeal of the "don't ask, don't tell" policy. Brass at Fort Bragg told CNN that they had no control over the spouse club because it's not a military group, but a private one.

Though gay people can now serve openly, the military doesn't formally recognize same-sex marriage under the federal Defense of Marriage Act [DOMA], a law passed in 1996 that denies many benefits to same-sex spouses. One of those benefits is military IDs.

The cards are an essential part of military life, allowing holders to get on base, access child care or go to the commissary.

Members-only Card

"The cards are also a big symbol," Broadway recalled. "So there I am listening to this person with this club tell me I can't join as I'm struggling to get my 2-year-old out of the car and into the house. And I just kept hearing over and over, 'You don't have an ID. You don't have an ID.' I was hearing it as, 'You are not equal. You are less.'"

Her voice breaks. "I kept thinking that if these people just met me, they would like me," she said, crying.

When Broadway hung up, she grabbed a laundry basket and began furiously folding clothes in her bedroom. She texted a friend who is also gay, also married to a service member and was himself in the military years ago.

"How can anyone not in our position know how this feels?" she asked.

By that night, she was just plain angry. No way was she just going to go away quietly.

Broadway posted an open letter to the club on the American Military Partner Association [AMPA], the nation's go-to support network for gay, lesbian and transgender military families.

Another Club Rejection

AMPA launched a petition not only for Broadway but also for other spouses who've tried and were barred from joining similar clubs, including Tanisha Ward.

Ward, who's married to a female Airman 1st Class, asked to join the Little Rock Spouses' Club near Little Rock Air Force Base in Jacksonville, Arkansas, in September [2012].

The club rejected Ward, she says, because she doesn't have a military-issued ID. But the group appears to be rethinking its stance.

Its website suggests the club might be considering new membership rules that a military ID card is not necessary to join, adding that no one should be blocked from membership because of sexual orientation.

Some of the other federal benefits that are available to married heterosexual couples but are denied to same-sex spouses include insurance and survivor's benefits.

"They've told me they're going to meet this month to decide," Ward said. "I hope they do the right thing."

But no luck for Broadway, whose name trended for weeks on Twitter. Her story is the talk in military circles, with *Stars and Stripes* [military newspaper] writing about it and Fort Bragg's community posting comments online.

"This is about more than a spouse who wants to get into a club," says UCLA [University of California Los Angeles] Law School's Aaron Belkin, who helped write the repeal of "don't ask, don't tell."

"This is about the Defense of Marriage Act and all the inequalities that come with it. It's about asking the question: Is the military really going to be serious about giving fair and equal treatment?"

Some of the other federal benefits that are available to married heterosexual couples but are denied to same-sex spouses include insurance and survivor's benefits. Straight spouses are able to file joint tax returns.

The U.S. Supreme Court will begin hearing arguments about the constitutionality of DOMA in March [2013].

A Spouse Is a Spouse

That offers little comfort to Broadway and her supporters, such as Bianca Strzalkowski, the 2011 Military Spouse of the Year. Hundreds of thousands of military members voted to give Strzalkowski that title, singling her out for her community service, patriotism and time spent helping military families. She lives in North Carolina but has no affiliation with the spouse club that rejected Broadway.

"It really makes me ill to think this is happening at Fort Bragg," she told CNN. "It's discrimination, plain and simple."

Strzalkowski is also the deputy membership director of Blue Star Families—the largest military family support organization in the nation. A Blue Star column recently lambasted the spouse club for rejecting Broadway.

"Who would have thought a group whose sole existence is to help other military spouses and families would deny one of their own? . . ." military wife Molly Blake wrote. "Ashley Broadway—I don't care if you are gay. I care that you are a dedicated military spouse who supports your soldier. I care that you want to be an example to other spouses and volunteer your time for the benefit of others.

We've gone through 11 years of war, and we need to be supporting each other—not treating each other like this.

"I care that you are willing to set up chairs and tables for fundraisers, bring new and innovative ways to raise money for our neediest military families, collate bid sheets, make brownies and raise your hand when the president needs a volunteer."

Strzalkowski's Marine husband is preparing to ship out on his fifth deployment, this time to Afghanistan.

"We've gone through 11 years of war, and we need to be supporting each other—not treating each other like this," she said. "I don't feel that this club at Fort Bragg represents who we are as spouses."

No Help from Bragg Brass

CNN's many attempts to get the club's side of the story have been unsuccessful. Two women who confirmed that they belonged to the club chose not to comment.

A December 12 [2012] letter on the club's home page reads: "In response to recent interest in the membership requirements of our organization we will review the issue at our next board meeting." The letter doesn't indicate when the meeting will be.

In the wake of the controversy, the group's website has password protected all its links. "They've locked themselves off to the world!" says Strzalkowski. "No one should be that high up on their pedestal."

Bragg brass says their power is limited. That's because, according to Fort Bragg Garrison Commander Col. Jeffrey Sanborn, the club is a private group, not a military one. Sanborn declined an interview with CNN, but he e-mailed statements saying he explained that in person to Broadway and her wife.

Officially, Sanborn has the power only to ensure "all private organizations operating on Fort Bragg comply with Department of Defense [DOD] and Army regulations and with U.S. laws."

And the spouse club's bylaws, constitution and conduct do comply with DOD regulations.

"C'mon, really? That's a little disingenuous," said UCLA's Belkin. "When you're the commander at Fort Bragg, you are close to having godlike status in your community."

Sanborn could deny the club access to the base, Belkin said.

"He could tell service members not to participate. There are a lot of ways to send a signal that you disapprove."

At home this week, Broadway and Mack are busy around the house. Mack is days away from giving birth. Broadway talks as she heads home from a visit to the doctor.

After all this, does Broadway still want to be part of the Association of Bragg Officers' Spouses?

"Honestly, I'm torn," she said. "Each day that goes by, they are saying they don't want me. I check my spam folder every day to make sure I haven't missed a message from them.

"I wonder if it would be best if I focus on a group who would value me."

When a Military Member Returns Home Family Readjustment May Be Difficult

Lydia I. Marek et al.

Lydia I. Marek is the lead author of the following viewpoint, which she wrote with eight other researchers. Marek is a research scientist in the department of human development at Virginia Tech. She is also a certified family life educator at the National Council on Family Relations and a licensed marriage and family therapist.

According to the Department of Defense, as of June 30, 2011, 203,400 military personnel, including reserve and National Guard members, were currently on deployment in Iraq or Afghanistan. As nearly one half of all military personnel are parents, and with almost two million children having a military parent, there are a growing number of families who are experiencing or have experienced the strain of wartime deployments. These deployments are characterized by lengthy and multiple separations that put stress on family functioning, structure, and cohesion. In addition, the effects of these deployments, with their related difficulties, can spill over into domains outside of the home and affect individual and social functioning. Military personnel, program providers, and helping professionals are becoming more interested in and concerned about the stage of deployment known as reintegration or postdeployment. Understanding this stage is especially important at this time, given the current drawdown of troops.

With the number of returning service members increasing, they and their families must now reassemble their lives after each member has experienced profound change.

Reintegration is the stage of the deployment cycle (predeployment, deployment, postdeployment or reintegration) characterized by the service member's reentry into his or her daily life as experienced prior to deployment, or into a new civilian life, including the domains of work, family, and personal experiences. Most often, this stage is another predeployment, given the operational tempo of the last 10 years; meaning that most service members are already preparing for another deployment immediately upon return to their families. Despite much literature suggesting that the reintegration stage lasts several months, this stage can actually persist for months to years depending on the individual service member, his or her family, and the fuller context of the service member's life. Notably, although many service members, spouses, and children or youth demonstrate great resilience during what can be a smooth and joyful reintegration process, many individuals and families have difficulties with this stage of deployment.

Reintegration can be a turbulent time for the family, as members must re-form into a functioning system. Some studies suggest that relationship stress and negative family function may reach a peak between 4 to 9 months after the service member's return. One of the greatest challenges for these families appears to be renegotiating family roles as the service member encounters the often-unexpected difficulty of fitting into a home routine that has likely changed a great deal since his or her departure. Typically, over the course of one or more deployments, the at-home parent and children (especially adolescents who are more capable of providing greater instrumental support within the home) assume new responsibilities such that when the service member returns, there may be expectations among family members that things will either return to how they were prior to deployment or that the structure that emerged during deployment will remain. Lack of appropriate expectations and communication around this restructuring is a frequent source of conflict and stress for reintegrating families.

Those involved with military families must understand the reintegration process and its effects on the service member and his or her family, because this multifaceted period of time has been found to have a profound impact on multiple life domains. With the current drawdown of troops in Iraq, this reintegration process is even more important for researchers and practitioners to understand so that critical supports for returning service members and their families can be developed, implemented, and evaluated. This article provides a brief overview of main issues in the process of reintegration for service members, spouses, children, and the family unit, and concludes with future research needs.

Some spouses report not having to adjust at all during reintegration while others report that their deployed partner is no longer the same person they knew previously.

Experience of Reintegration

During the service member's reentry to the home, he or she faces physical, psychological (e.g., symptoms related to an experience of trauma), and social challenges. [A.B.] Adler, [M.] Zamorski, and [T.W.] Britt (2011) suggested a model of service member transition in which the effect of deployment-related variables (deployment experiences, anticipation of homecoming, and meaningfulness) on domains of postdeployment transition (physical, emotional, and social) are moderated by the service member's decompression, or the psychological transition from functioning in a high-stress and pressure-filled environment to one of less stress and pressure (in other words, the psychological processes involved in going from battlefield to bedroom), his or her personal narrative around military experiences, unit variables, and the anticipation of redeployment. These transition domains can then directly affect the quality of one's health, work, relationships, and an overall ability to enjoy life. Studies have identified specific challenges facing reintegrating service members as follows:

1. Feeling like they no longer fit into their families due to the family changes that occurred in their absence, including the normative development and maturation of children and the increased competence of the spouse who has taken over many of the tasks and roles that were previously completed by the service member.

2. A feeling of separation for returning service members from the culture to which they return. Several reasons were cited such as lack of respect from civilians (including a loss of status and self-esteem), the belief that they hold themselves to a higher standard than civilians, and the complexity of "normal" life.

Reintegration can be a very difficult time for children and youth.

---

3. Difficulties related to interpersonal interactions (including those with their partners and children) due to low frustration tolerance, poor anger management, difficulties in coping and self-regulation, hypervigilance, and social withdrawal. Many of these could be characterized as post-traumatic stress symptoms and may also include increased alcohol use and heightened symptoms of depression and anxiety.

Spouses of Service Members

[S.H.] Pincus, [R.] House, [J.] Christensen, and [L.E.] Adler (2001) postulated that postdeployment is arguably the most important stage for the service member and spouse as they often must reduce expectations, take time to become reacquainted with one another, and build communication. Reactions to the return of the deployed service member can vary wildly; some spouses report not having to adjust at all during reintegration while others report that their deployed partner is no longer the same person they knew previously, making for a rather difficult adjustment. Despite the potential for positive effects of reintegration (e.g., greater appreciation for one's family, personal growth), spouses may experience a loss of the independence gained during the service member's deployment and the loss of the social support networks formed during that time. [A.] Chandra and colleagues (2011) found the following challenges expressed by spouses related to reintegration:

1. Fitting the deployed spouse back into the home routine;

2. Rebalancing child responsibilities;

3. Getting to know the deployed spouse again;

4. Worrying about the next deployment;

5. Dealing with the deployed spouse's mood changes; and

6. Deciding who to turn to for advice.

Some mitigating factors that are associated with the reintegration process include frequency of contact during deployment, overall adjustment to deployment, use of military support programs, and age of children. Negative communications with the service member, negative beliefs in the value of the service member's mission, and the service member's exposure to combat were significant predictors of wives' stress during postdeployment. Making sense of the deployment process in general and making appropriate attributions of the military partner's behavior in particular (e.g., if trauma symptoms are present) are valuable in reducing reintegration stress.

Military Children/Youth

Reintegration can be a very difficult time for children and youth. While proud of their deployed parent, many report feelings of loss, loneliness, and worry for the safety of their military parent during deployment and frequently must take on more responsibilities in the home. The child or youth may eagerly anticipate reconnecting with the service member parent who returns. Nevertheless, both parent and child may have undergone significant changes during deployment, thus heightening the unpredictability of this time for everyone.

Although a majority of families make the appropriate adaptations during postdeployment and demonstrate a great degree of resilience, many report difficulties.

A variety of factors, such as a child's stage of development (emotional, cognitive, or physical), the at-home caregiver's satisfaction with military and community support, the individual adjustment and emotional development of the parents, and the degree of marital stability can all affect a child's adjustment to reunion and reintegration. Studies have found that children and youth expressed difficulty relating to the reintegrating parent due to the physical, mental, and emotional changes that resulted from deployment. Children reportedly expected increased parental attention during reintegration and often did not understand why they did not receive it. Youth adjustment may be moderated by age, gender, and cumulative length of deployment, such that older girls who experienced longer parental deployments were at greater risk for reintegration difficulties. Boys, on the other hand, may have more difficulty adjusting to reduced autonomy and increased structure when the deployed parent returns home.

In spite of their challenges, many children demonstrate remarkable resilience during deployment and reintegration. Chandra and colleagues (2011) reported that when concerns did arise, they tended to focus on:

1. Adjusting to fit the deployed parent back into the home routine;

2. Worrying about the next deployment;

3. Dealing with the service member's mood changes;

4. Worrying about how parents are getting along;

5. Becoming reacquainted with the service member; and

6. Deciding who to turn to for support and advice.

Military Families

Family adjustment depends on a variety of factors, and although a majority of families make the appropriate adaptations during postdeployment and demonstrate a great degree of resilience, many report difficulties. The family dynamics created during deployment are often challenged during reintegration. Mechanisms of risk for these families, identified by [W.R.] Saltzman and colleagues (2011), include:

1. An incomplete understanding of the impact of deployment and combat operational stress;

2. Inaccurate developmental expectations;

3. Impaired family communication;

4. Impaired parenting practices;

5. Impaired family organization; and

6. A lack of a guiding belief system (i.e., values or beliefs that enable a family to make sense of and find meaning in their circumstances or a difficult situation).

[S.H.] Pincus and colleagues (2011) also suggest that there are a number of adaptations that can serve as protective factors and ease the family into the reintegration process. These include:

1. Being able to have role flexibility with the ability to perform multiple roles;

2. Using active coping skills;

3. Maintaining contact through e-mail and letter writing during deployment;

4. Having all family members maintain realistic expectations during this reintegration process;

5. Developing a shared family narrative and collaborative meaning-making;

6. Open communication in the family; and

7. Effective parental leadership.

Next Steps

Our current knowledge of reintegration experiences, how they unfold over time, and their consequences is for the most part based on research using largely clinical samples focusing on service member experiences of post-traumatic stress disorder and its impact on the marital relationship and parenting. Such a focus obscures the fact that even in the absence of formal mental health diagnoses for service members, difficulties can and do arise, thus warranting further research with nonclinical samples. There is a need for a greater balance between strengths-based or family resilience approaches and those emphasizing psychopathology and its transmission. Other limits of reintegration research thus far include the following:

1. Many service members have been surveyed about their experiences of reintegration years after returning from deployment (rather than during or immediately following postdeployment);

2. Measures used have reported limited psychometric information;

3. Most current research is cross-sectional with some notable exceptions;

4. Data are seldom gathered from multiple informants; and

5. There is insufficient attention to theory, thereby limiting the application and building of family stress and resilience research and understanding.

Addressing these deficits would enrich our knowledge of the process of reintegration and help highlight the stressors and resilience factors in military families. More research that is family-focused and longitudinal, using nonclinical samples and measures that have demonstrated psychometrics, is needed. This understanding could then lead to the development, implementation, and evaluation of effective support programs and services targeted at each of these groups during specific time periods. Strong and effective collaboration between the military and civilian community would be needed for such a research agenda and is essential if we are to assist in building the resiliency of military families during the potentially difficult and multidimensional process of reintegration.

Trouble on the Home Front

Kathy Roth-Douquet

Kathy Roth-Douquet is the chief executive officer of Blue Star Families, a national military family organization. She is a former government official, a practicing attorney, an author, and a military spouse.

Are my fellow military wives and I shocked and outraged by General Petraeus' adultery? Frankly, after 11 years of war, military families around bases and posts throughout the world are too tired for shock, too experienced for outrage over this unhappy episode. I've heard a range of reactions, from sad recognition, to compassion, to the knowing response that no one can look inside another person's marriage. This story does, almost universally, make us reflect on the strains our families have been through over the past 11 years, and the fact that in many ways, the strains are about to get worse.

Yes, worse.

It is wonderful that the war in Iraq is over, that the war in Afghanistan will wind down in 2014. Sing hallelujah, strew the eucalyptus. It has been a difficult time for many men, women, children, and marriages. That's not the whole story—many marriages stand strong for the joint experience of having been called to do something difficult, and meeting the call. Many marriages took a heavy challenge, but fought back. I think of my friend who, in the airport after the welcome home "honeymoon" with her Special Forces husband, opened an email with pictures of him and another woman. She left her husband, but eventually they came back together, and with counseling confronted together the strain of repeated combat and his destructive choice to cope through affairs. In fact, despite extraordinary challenges, military couples are still no more likely to divorce than similar civilians. But statistics shouldn't mislead anyone to think that things are therefore fine.

It is very difficult for civilians to appreciate what the past decade-plus has been like for so many of our military families. Half of those responding to the Blue Star Families annual Military Family Lifestyle Survey have been separated from their spouse for more than *two years*. Half of those families have been separated for more than four years—not only for combat and non-combat deployments, but for schools, trainings, and temporary assignments.

What happens during those years apart? Births, deaths, personal growth, trauma. As one friend of mine explained to me, "When my husband left for his first deployment, we were basically newlyweds. Three years later after back-to-back deployments and 'temporary duty' assignments he came home to find me, this single mother of a special needs child who didn't recognize him."

For the active duty military and their families, war—or war-like readiness—is going to continue as a way of life. There's no peace dividend for military families.

It's not just the separation; it's also the reintegration after the stress of combat. Over a quarter of the military spouses in the BSF survey reported seeing symptoms of Post Traumatic Stress in their service member (with less than half seeking and receiving a diagnosis). That squares with the Veterans Affairs estimate that 11–20 percent of Iraq and Afghanistan veterans experience PTSD. Almost a fifth in the survey said that reintegration with spouse and children after deployment was difficult or very difficult. Add the difficulty of reunion to the fact that the average military child moves 6–9 times.

Another friend of mine tells of her Marine husband's anger and how her son, dealing with moves and his father's rage, spiraled down in school. Her husband retired from the military, and the marriage fell apart. She loves her ex-husband, and still wonders about reconciling—on the other hand, her son is doing much better. It's hard to know what the right thing is to do in these situations.

But, one might say, Iraq is over, Afghanistan winding down. Problem solved, right?

Wrong, because for the active duty military and their families, war—or war-like readiness—is going to continue as a way of life. There's no peace dividend for military families. It's something the civilian society should be aware of, because as government resources dwindle, we'll need support to help us continue to cope.

Cope with what? Set aside the very pertinent fact that we still have 68,000 troops in Afghanistan. The U.S. military is forward-deployed, away from family, throughout Africa, in the Balkans and Black Sea, around the Middle East, in South America, on ships in the Pacific, around the straights of Malaca, in Korea. We send and will continue to send thousands of service members to Japan on *two-year* orders away from their families. We will add new deployments to places like, Australia.

Our military understands that family strength is a component of readiness, because if military life is too hard on families, we can no longer retain our force.

To many military planners, the world is no less dangerous now than it has been—it is perhaps even more dangerous. The Army is planning to move to a faster, cheaper rotational force, increasing "responsiveness and mobility" according to Army plans and policy. This means some Army families used to being together in garrison for two to three years in the United States will now live more like the Marine Corps, with their service member leaving them for six months or more at a time for "peacetime deployments" as part of the new way of doing business.

Here's how Secretary Panetta describes the post-Iraq-and-Afghanistan missions of this "smaller, leaner" force: they will counter terrorism and irregular warfare, deter and defeat aggression, project power despite external challenges, counter weapons of mass destruction, defend the homeland, provide a stabilizing presence throughout key areas of the globe, conduct stability and counterinsurgency operations, and conduct humanitarian, disaster relief, and other operations.

Suffice it to say, our military will be busy. The families will continue to feel that they are at war—but they will not have the same level of public backing that they have been able to rely on. As much of a strain as the hot wars were, they had in their way become predictable. Most families had long notice before their loved ones left, and they left in large units with significant support, including family readiness officers. The new force will be smaller, the separations will be less predictable, and there will be less support. Paychecks will be smaller since combat-zone tax-free pay and extra combat pay will go away; and the declining budget means fewer military-sponsored family programs. Plus, American society at large will think that the war is over, the troops have come home.

Why should Americans care? Because families remain a key partner in the health and stability of our military. Our military understands that family strength is a component of readiness, because if military life is too hard on families, we can no longer retain our force. Moreover, when the troops are in distress, families are a key line of defense. Finally, the country should care because in the end the military and the families serve the nation, not the Pentagon. We've had unprecedented support in recent years during the wars. And we still need it. If the media and Washington gave a fraction of the attention to this issue as they have to David Petraeus, we could perhaps mobilize a response to this coming challenge. And that could make a difference to our families, to our military, even to our national security.

CONTROVERSIES

CHAPTER 3

Is Being Part of a Military Family Detrimental to Children?

Chapter Preface

A good deal of recent research has shown that children of military families, especially those in which a parent is deployed, are at greater than average risk of social, behavioral, and mental health problems. This is true even of very young children, although the risk of such problems increases with age. It has been found that military kids seek mental health care and are admitted to hospitals more frequently than civilians, and there are even more cases of attempted suicide.

Because military bases provide a support network for families and their children are in close contact with others in similar circumstances, those who live there are less likely to have emotional problems than those who live off-base. But the majority of military families do not live in base housing, and people within the community, as well as teachers in its schools, do not always understand what a military child is going through. They may not be aware of situations where extra help is needed, and the family may not seek out the organizations that offer it until problems have developed.

Children are affected not only by missing absent parents and worrying about their safety, but by the emotional turmoil of the parent who remains. Spouses separated from loved partners cannot help revealing their feelings, even if they don't talk about them—and of course, they often do. Tensions within the family build up, and for some children, this leads to serious depression or other mental health disorders. Such problems can be lasting, particularly if the deployed parent has Post-Traumatic Stress Disorder (PTSD) or other health issues when he or she returns and has difficulty getting back to a normal way of life.

Even when military parents are not deployed, frequent moves often result in problems for their children, who are forced to leave their friends and may have difficulty adjusting to new schools. Often, they no sooner get settled in one place than they are torn away again. Their school performance may suffer; also, some engage in violent behavior such as fighting, while others become depressed and withdrawn.

All of this is understandable, considering the amount of stress military children experience, for both mental and physical health problems are often caused by stress. What may be more surprising is that although such problems are more common among military kids than in civilian families, the majority do not have them. Most military children remain healthy despite the stress they are under, and many are more self-sufficient and better adjusted than average. Dealing successfully with challenging situations tends to make people stronger, and this is certainly true of military families, as is frequently recognized by observers.

Air Force Master Sergeant Jeffrey Moody, a military dad, wrote, "My children are resilient. They withstand every separation or move, we recover as a reunited family, and they grow by experiencing these challenges first hand. Their ability to bounce back is truly inspiring."

"Dandelions can take root almost anywhere, and they are almost impossible to destroy," said Colonel Robert A. Barker, garrison commander at Fort Gordon in Augusta, Georgia, at a school celebration of the 2013 Month of the Military Child. "Like the dandelions, military children bloom everywhere the winds carry them. They are hardy and upright. Their roots are strong, and cultivated deeply in the culture of the military. They are ready to fly in the winds that take them to new adventures, new lands, and new friends."

"Military children are well-rounded, culturally aware, tolerant, and extremely resilient," he added. "They have learned from an early age that home is where their hearts are, that a good friend can be found in every corner of the world and in every color, and that education does not only come from school, but also by living in the history that surrounds them every day."

Children of Military Families Experience Stress That Affects School Performance

Gabrielle Canon

Gabrielle Canon is a journalist whose work has been featured in several publications and who was assistant producer for a syndicated talk radio program focusing on politics, the environment, and international affairs.

Michelle Hurley attended 12 different schools in six different states by the time she reached her high school graduation. She shifted between three different schools during her high school years alone.

"You just learn to deal with it," she says. "I was in the third grade before I did a full year of school without moving."

This is the reality children with parents in the military continue to face each year.

Hurley was on the move often, following her father, who was on active duty in the Army during her childhood. As he was reassigned, his faithful family followed, each time having to build new relationships and adjust to new surroundings.

Hurley remembers the frustration that came with each move and the fear that came with the midnight phone calls. Usually the wives of fellow military men called her mother for late-night support, relying on the solace of sharing their situation with others. She remembers how difficult it was when her father was gone, serving in the first Iraq war.

"You end up relying on your family to get you through," she recalls. "You just lean on each other."

According to the Department of Defense, there are currently over 2 million children of military parents in the United States. Military children typically attend between seven to nine schools before they graduate, moving approximately every two years. Each relocation brings with it the numerous problems associated with transitioning between education systems that may not translate. All these issues Robert Blum, professor of the Johns Hopkins Bloomberg School of Public Health elaborated in an interview with the American Association of School Administrators (AASA), about the difficulties children face when forced to live this lifestyle.

> Military families and military children are amongst the most transient of populations. It is not uncommon to see kids who have grown up in military families who have been in 5, 7 or 9 different schools by the end of their high school career. There is very high mobility. With high mobility comes issues of engagement, disengagement and reengagement.

Older children, who understand the reality and potential dangers associated with their parent's absence, exhibit signs of fear, irritability and sometimes aggression.

How High Mobility Affects Children

The Department of Defense found that children at different stages of development are affected in different ways.

Children ages 3 through 6 were found to exhibit behaviors of stress including regression, physical complaints and fears of separation.

Older children, who understand the reality and potential dangers associated with their parent's absence, exhibit signs of fear, irritability and sometimes aggression.

Teenagers were found to be rebellious and at higher risk of using drugs and engaging in early-age sexual behavior.

All of these emotional responses can have grave implications on academic performance.

In an effort to facilitate better understanding of the issues facing military children, the RAND Center for Military Health and Policy Research released a study entitled "Effects of Soldiers' Deployment on Children's Academic Performance and Behavioral Health."

The report found,

> Long and frequent deployments, with short dwell times in between, have placed stresses on Army children and families already challenged by frequent moves and parental absences. These stresses may present in the form of social, emotional, or behavioral problems among children at home and at school.

According to the study, the longer parental deployments were, the larger the impact on child academic achievement. Children who participated in the study were found to have lower achievement scores when their parents had deployed 19 months or more since 2001, across all academic subjects.

Support for School-Age Military Children

In light of these troubling findings, government bodies and nonprofit organizations alike are searching for solutions to help support school-age military children.

One government initiative that has resulted in recent years is the Interstate Compact on Educational Opportunity for Military Children, which was created in 2008.

The compact identified further issues affecting students,

> Military children often experience delayed enrollment, inappropriate grade-level placement, exclusion from educational programs and extracurricular activities, and delayed graduation. The compact establishes guidelines to better enable member states to address these issues.

Developed by the Council of State Governments, the compact seeks to align standards in education across the nation, including issues with enrollment, placement and attendance, and eligibility for extracurricular activities, to ease the difficulties associated with relocation and help a greater number of military children graduate on time.

According to AASA, 18 months after its creation, 26 states had signed onto the compact and, as a result, affecting 70 percent of school-aged military children.

Other programs have also been developed to assist these children academically. Student Online Achievement Resources (SOAR), provides online resources that allows students to sign on, take assessment tests based on state standards, and follow personalized tutorials. According to their website the program also allows parents to view their child's results from anywhere.

> SOAR is an innovative program that makes it easy for parents to play an active role in their children's education. SOAR is designed for military families, and is easily accessible worldwide.

Tutor.com has also offered their services to the military for free. Tutor.com is an online resource that provides access to professional tutors, day or night.

These programs are providing solutions to many of the problems military children face, however, experts say more needs to be done.

"More resources are available now than there have ever been, but we are dealing with the cumulative stress of a decade at war," says Joyce Wessel Raezer, the Executive Director of The National Military Family Association (NMFA).

"I believe what is going to be needed is sustained support," she elaborates. "Everyone across the country needs to realize the legacy of war is still there and it will stay with this nation for a very long time."

The Need for Civilian Community Help

NMFA has created several programs, not only to assist families in the military, but also to provide resources for civilian members of the community who are needed to ensure these families are able to acclimate. "Finding Common Ground: A Toolkit for Communities Supporting Military Families," is a publication featured on their website that outlines several solutions civilians can take to lend a hand.

Civilian communities will make the key difference in assisting America's heroes and their families.

According to the publication, 70 percent of military families live in civilian communities. This is why it is essential for these neighborhoods to understand the needs of military families.

According to "Best Practices in Enhancing School Environment," a report commissioned by the Department of Defense, non-military schools should be better equipped to handle students with parents in the military, and experts believe this could be one of the most important factors in the success of these students.

> A positive school environment creates an optimal setting for teaching and learning. Research shows that school can be a stabilizing force for young people, both emotionally and academically, particularly when they are experiencing transition or crisis.

Michelle Hurley was lucky to be able to navigate the stressful life of the military child successfully. She reflects on her past, finding positivity in the struggles she faced. "It made me independent," she says, "and shaped the person I am today."

Though she was able to rely on the foundation her family provided, others may falter. Programs and resources are providing solutions, but civilian communities will make the key difference in assisting America's heroes and their families.

"Families are strong, but they are tired and stressed," Raezer says. "Communities need to learn how to help, because it takes all of us to support that military family."

Frequent Moves Create Many Problems for Adolescents in Military Families

Catherine P. Bradshaw et al.

Catherine P. Bradshaw cowrote the following viewpoint with three other researchers at the Johns Hopkins Bloomberg School of Public Health. Bradshaw is an associate professor in the department of mental health at the School of Public Health, as well as the deputy director of the Johns Hopkins Center for Prevention of Youth Violence.

A cross all three groups (students, parents, and school staff), a set of themes emerged as stressors that resulted from being a part of the military culture. The data indicated that the most prevalent stressors on the students resulted from tension at home, strains on their relationships with peers, adapting to a new school environment, academic challenges, student/teacher relationships, and becoming involved in extracurricular activities.

Stress on the Family System

A common concern expressed across all groups—parents, students, and staff—was the effect of military-related moves on the family's experience of stress. The unpredictable nature of the moves seemed to be particularly problematic.

> You want to stay with your family and you want to be with them, but sometimes the military moves you at the wrong time—either when everything is great or when everything sucks. (student)

Catherine P. Bradshaw, May Sudhimaraset, Kristin Mmari, and Robert W. Blum, "School Transitions Among Military Adolescents: A Qualitative Study of Stress and Coping," *School Psychology Review*, Spring, 2010. Copyright 2010 by the National Association of School Psychologists. Bethesda, MD. Reprinted with permission of the publisher. www.nasponline.org.

A common theme among the students was that relocation increased tension in the family. Some students said they experienced anger toward their parents and the military because of the frequent relocations and disruptions resulting from their parents' involvement in the military. Several students reported "protesting" the move; as one student explained, "I think every military kid has said that 'I'm not moving.'" Both students and parents described situations where the student ran away from home in protest of the move:

> My daughter is in the fourth grade and she has been in 11 different schools. She refuses to make friends because we are moving again. She says, "I'm not doing it." And my son, in fact we just got orders again, and I told him . . . we are moving again, and he ran away. He said, "I'm running away. I don't want to move ever again." So I think it is really truly difficult on them, especially when it is short moves. It really impacts them—more than if you stay someplace for 2 or 3 years. Because they get to create that base and have a safe home base. Whereas they [the military] move you someplace and the chances are you're moving again in 12 months. They are not going to set roots down, because they know [they are going to move again]. (parent) . . .

The process of trying to break into established social networks was . . . difficult for many of the students.

Stress on the Students' Social Support System

One commonly mentioned stressor associated with frequent relocations was the challenge of initiating and sustaining close friendships. In fact, many students described how difficult it was for them when they had to separate from their long-time friends. One male student commented, "Once you start getting close with friends and everything, it [moving] just gets harder and harder and harder." Another student described the negative effect of moving on friendships:

> The moving can be really hard. I had friends at another school that I was growing up with and everything was going okay. And then I moved to another school [where] I'm the new kid. It was hard to make friends. Then it happened again when I was starting to settle down. (student)

Another concern described by students was their perception of change in their friends' behaviors toward them as a result of their multiple moves. They described how their friends would "act different" or pull away from them in preparation for an upcoming move. The process of trying to break into established social networks was also difficult for many of the students. One student stated, "Having to move in the middle of a school year [is difficult]. People already have new little cliques, and whatever. It is hard to get people to invite you in and meet people."

> It is really hard moving to a different high school because everyone already has their cliques. Everyone already has their friends and you are coming in from a different place. You don't really know anybody. (student)

Parents confirmed many of the challenges that the adolescents expressed with regard to forming and maintaining friendships. Moreover, military students who live on base also have military friends who are likely to experience multiple relocations.

> I think another thing that they [students] worry about, not only making friends, but losing them too. I mean, I could not believe when she started kindergarten that she would come home. There would be this snack calendar and then the next month there would be like three kids gone from the calendar. "Well he moved away, his daddy had to go to a different job and they moved, and they moved, and they moved" . . . I mean I think it is hard on them losing their friends. They worry about losing them as much as they worry about getting them. (parent)

One parent, who also was a service member, commented on the anxiety his adolescent children experienced related to frequent moves, and how it was similar to his own experience as a military student. Particularly striking was his description of the long-term effect of these transitions on his own ability to form intimate relationships.

> That is an anxiety that they have. I know, being a military brat [myself]. My dad was Air Force. So I know what it is like to try to get friends and relationships and stuff. I am still having problems with relationships because I have always been that same way. . . . I always went to off-base schools. But you never knew when you were going to move. . . . So it is just that relationship thing, it is a dual [edged] sword. One thing is that they learn to adapt, but the other thing is they are scared to commit to a relationship because they don't know when they are going to move again. (parent)

Although one adolescent discussed "the respect you get for being in the military," others reported feeling discriminated against because of their military status.

Adapting to a New Context and Environment

Although the students reported that much of the stress experienced at school was associated with their social networks, there were some added stressors resulting from aspects of the new school environment, such as adjusting to the physical building, adapting to the culture and context of the school and the broader community, and learning the school's policies and procedures. The unpredictability of the new school environment was described as being particularly stressful for the students. . . .

Both students and school staff agreed that the timing of the move tends to affect the student's transition into a new school. Military students who move in the middle of a school year may experience added stressors such as assimilating into already established cliques, learning the layout of a new school, and school credit issues. School staff also observed these changes, as one noted, "Freshmen and sophomores [who] transfer in, I have seen it is easier for them to fall in and get in line."

> I left senior year, and so I had to start all over in a new school, with like a new environment and everything. It was really hard to get into the school and get to know people. Whereas if I was staying in Germany I would have been like, "hey, I know everybody here." That was one of the really hard things—moving my senior year and just having 3 years there, and then having to move. (student)

The students also reported facing an interesting mix of both positive and negative stereotypes of "military brats." Although one adolescent discussed "the respect you get for being in the military," others reported feeling discriminated against because of their military status.

> I think it would be really helpful if other students didn't make first impressions about you, like they just see you and say, "oh she is an Army child. She is probably different. She probably doesn't have very many friends, so we have to stay away from her." So, if people would actually get to know you better than just first impressions, it would be a lot more helpful. (student)

After moving from one school to another, high school students may not be able to complete all the graduation requirements in time.

Other students talked about the pressure to meet the exceptionally high expectations that their teachers, parents, and peers had of them. One parent commented on teachers' high expectations for their newly transitioned military students: "They expect the children to assimilate, rather than having an understanding that they are different—find a niche for them. They want the children to assimilate and I think that is inappropriate."

Academic Challenges

There were numerous challenges and concerns raised in relation to academics and the quality of the educational services. Issues raised across all focus groups included quality of education, differences in school requirements and the implications of frequently moving, children with special needs, and school size. For parents, their primary concern was the quality of educational services provided to military students. As one parent reported, "My biggest fear for my child when we moved is that he is not getting a proper education and I do not know how to do it for him." Students and parents reported several academic problems and challenges resulting from the frequent school transitions. These problems ranged from having to repeat classes and lessons to missing critical topics, such as fractions, multiplication, and cursive handwriting. Many of the parents reported trying to help fill in these gaps, but not all parents had the time or expertise to do this. . . .

Both parents and students discussed the concern that after moving from one school to another, high school students may not be able to complete all the graduation requirements in time. In fact, a couple of the adolescent focus group participants reported that they or their friends had to stay in high school an extra year to complete all the requirements for graduation. The students reported that repeating these courses—or worse yet, being delayed a year—had a negative effect on their self-esteem, attitudes toward school, and academic motivation.

> Every state has different graduation requirements and I had to come here and I had to take freshman classes because . . .

that is what you needed to graduate here.... That kind of pays a toll because you can't take the classes you want. You can't be successful in different things. You have to go by guidelines of the different state. You feel pretty stupid. (student)

Parents of children with special needs, such as learning disabilities, were especially concerned with the support services available and testing process upon relocation. As one parent described,

It doesn't matter if your kid is advanced, behind, [has] learning disabilities, or whatever. When you transfer from state to state or school to school or whatever it is, it takes forever. They want to retest them, the [same] test that your kid just went through six months ago. [They say], "Oh we want to retest them here." I have a child who had a learning disability and it took me 2 years [to get him services] because we moved from school to school. Everyone wanted to retest him, everyone had a different theory, everyone had different ideas. And then he transferred. We bring all the transcripts for the testing and documentation [to the new school], and they say, "We are going to do our own testing on him." My kid suffered for 2 years. (parent)...

Student/Teacher Relationships

The way in which school staff members interact with military students can either buffer or exacerbate the stress that students experience. This issue is particularly salient for students who have a parent who is deployed. School staff reported great difficulty determining the "right thing" to do and say to military students regarding their parents' service or deployment. The students' perceptions of the "right thing" to do and say about their parents' involvement in the military or deployment status varied considerably. Some students did not want to draw attention to themselves, whereas others wanted to talk with other students and their teachers about their concerns or share stories about their parents' military-related accomplishments. This likely makes it difficult for teachers and other staff to know how to handle the issue or respond appropriately. . . .

A very common challenge experienced by military students was becoming involved in extracurricular activities.

Several parents described the "hit or miss" process of getting teachers who understand the unique needs of military students.

> Every once and a while I have found a teacher that is genuinely interested in dealing with my child because of the military background and understanding that they move around and there is so much diversity. And there is so much adjustment for them—they will go the extra mile to help. But I don't know, overall, I don't know. I think there is disconnection there a lot of times. (parent)

Several parents commented that all teachers working with military students, particularly off-base schools, need additional training in how to support military students. "They don't know how to deal with military children and deployments and things like that. They need to be educated on that more," one parent stated.

Missed Opportunities for Extracurricular Activities

A very common challenge experienced by military students was becoming involved in extracurricular activities, such as sports and student government associations. Participants across all focus group types (students, parents, and staff) described how difficult it was for transitioning military students to "break into" these established groups and networks.

> It is hard to get into sports, hard to get involved in school and stuff. So that kind of changes you a little bit. Because

you were really involved where you used to live, and then you come somewhere, and it is like a red line. I mean, you can't do anything. It is hard to get onto sports teams—you know, that type of thing. (student)

In fact, several parents and students reported that their military status may pose a greater challenge in becoming involved in extracurricular activities. Student and parent participants both reported that athletic coaches were hesitant to put military students on teams—particularly in starting positions—for fear of disrupting the team or losing the starting player to a military-related move. The students were also sensitive to the effect of gaining or losing a team member because of a military-related transition. One student described how turnover on the team affected the "bonding" and the team's performance: "It is hard on the sports side because you are moving from team to team and you don't get the usual bonding that you would if you stayed in one spot." The timing of the move can also influence the student's eligibility to participate in sports and other extracurricular activities. Students who move to a school late in the year often miss tryouts for the teams. It can also create animosity among the students when a "star" athlete transfers into the school, "stealing" a critical position from an established player. . . .

Furthermore, the number of extracurricular activities offered in a given school varies across districts and the time of year. For example, smaller communities or schools may offer fewer opportunities for certain sports, like ice hockey or gymnastics, as opposed to larger metropolitan areas. One student described how his school's sports teams and division limited his ability to leverage a college sports scholarship.

I think it is also hard, like with sports, scholarship-wise, because most D1 [Division 1] schools and stuff like that are looking at the big schools, rather than looking at a small school on base, like a 2A school like ours. I think that is kind of difficult sometimes. (student)

Military students also face challenges getting involved in other types of extracurricular activities, such as student government associations, which rely heavily on students' name recognition, history of service in the school, and overall popularity. Both types of activities share the commonality of limiting opportunities for military students to reach high-status positions, or a potential loss of status when a move is initiated. The situation is slightly different for other noncompetitive extracurricular activities, such as clubs. Most clubs are not exclusive, and thus transfers can join at any time; therefore, these types of activities are perceived as a potential networking opportunity and were often sought out by military students.

Children of Deployed Military Personnel Often Have Mental Health Problems

Kimberly Hefling

Kimberly Hefling is a writer for the Associated Press.

After nearly eight years of war, soldiers are not the only ones experiencing mental anguish. Their children are, too.

Last year [2008], children of U.S. troops sought outpatient mental health care 2 million times—double the number at the start of the Iraq war. There was also an alarming spike in the number of military kids actually hospitalized for mental health reasons.

Internal Pentagon documents show the increases, which come as the services struggle with wars in Iraq and Afghanistan and a shortage of therapists.

From 2007 to 2008, some 20 percent more children of active duty troops were hospitalized for mental health services, the documents show. Since the 2003 invasion of Iraq, inpatient visits among military children have increased 50 percent.

The total number of outpatient mental health visits for children of men and women on active duty doubled from 1 million in 2003 to 2 million in 2008. During the same period, the yearly bed days for military children 14 and under increased from 35,000 to 55,000, the documents show.

Overall, the number of children and spouses of active duty personnel and Guard and Reserve troops seeking mental health care has been steadily increasing. Last year's increase in child hospitalizations coincided with the "surge" of tens of thousands of additional U.S. troops into Iraq to stabilize the country.

However, reasons for the treatment increases are not clear from the documents. Besides the impact of service members' repeated tours in overseas war zones—and the severe economic recession that has affected all American families—the military has been encouraging troops' family members to seek mental health help when needed.

The military plans additional research.

Still, the statistics seem to reinforce the concerns of military leaders and private family organizations about the strains of the wars. Along with issues of separation, some families must deal with injuries or the deaths of loved ones.

Military families move, on average, nearly every three years, which adds additional stress.

"Army families are stretched, and they are stressed," Sheila Casey, wife of Gen. George W. Casey Jr., the U.S. Army chief of staff, told a congressional panel last month. "And I have often referred to them as the most brittle part of the force."

In the long run, you have to wonder if there isn't going to be detrimental effects that might hang on for a long period of time.

Troubling Signs

Evidence of domestic violence and child neglect among military families, as well as an increase in suicide, alcohol abuse and cases of post-traumatic stress, are all troubling signs, Mrs. Casey told a Senate Armed Services subcommittee. She and other military spouses testified that gaining access to mental health care is a problem.

At summer camps organized by the National Military Family Association for about 10,000 children, most of them kids of deployed soldiers, there have been more anecdotal reports this year of young people taking medication and showing signs of severe homesickness, anxiety, or depression, said Patricia Barron, who runs the association's youth initiatives.

Barron, a military spouse, said her organization is participating in a study on deployments and families. She said much is still unknown about the effects.

"If it continues to happen, you have to wonder how this is affecting them," Barron said. "In the long run, you have to wonder if there isn't going to be detrimental effects that might hang on for a long period of time."

The shortage of mental health professionals isn't just isolated to the military. But the problem is more pronounced because of the increase in demand, both on the home front and in the war zones.

About 20 percent to 30 percent of service members returning from war report some form of psychological distress.

There are efforts under way to encourage the military, the Veterans Affairs Department and state and local agencies to share mental health resources. Also, there have been incentives offered to encourage military spouses to enter easily transferrable fields such as health care.

In recent years, there's been an increase in funding in areas such as education, housing and child care devoted to improving the quality of life for military families. First lady Michelle Obama has said helping military families is a priority.

Violent Behavior Is More Common Among Military Children than Among Others

Mike Stobbe

Mike Stobbe is a medical writer for the Associated Press.

A new study suggests that when parents are deployed in the military, their children are more than twice as likely to carry a weapon, join a gang or be involved in fights.

And that includes the daughters.

"This study raises serious concerns about an under-recognized consequence of war," said Sarah Reed, who led the research of military families in Washington state.

Last year, nearly 2 million U.S. children had at least one parent serving in the military. Deployment can hurt a family in a variety of ways. There's stress while that parent is overseas and in danger, as the remaining parent has to shoulder all responsibilities and family roles shift. There can also be challenges after deployed parents' return, especially if they were physically or psychologically damaged.

The effect of military deployment on kids is an emerging field of research. The new study is considered the first of its kind to focus on those affected by deployments to Afghanistan and Iraq. It's unique in that it looked at a statewide swath of the population in comparing the behavior of kids in military families to children in non-military families.

The study, to be presented Monday [October 31, 2011] at a public health conference in Washington, D.C., was based on a 2008 questionnaire survey of about 10,000 students in the

8th, 10th and 12th grades in Washington [state]. That state has the sixth largest active duty population in the country.

About 550 of surveyed children said they had a parent deployed to a combat zone in the previous six years.

The study tried to account for potential differences in educational background and other issues between military families and the general population that might skew the results.

> The new research may be something of a wake-up call for health professionals who deal with military families.

Even after taking steps to account for such differences, the researchers found that high school-age daughters of deployed parents were nearly three times more likely than civilian girls to be in a gang or get into a fight. They were more than twice as likely to carry a weapon to school. There were similar increases among boys of deployed families when compared to civilians.

To be sure, such behavior in boys is more common—the rate of boys from deployed families involved in such violent behaviors was twice as high as for girls in deployed families. For example, 14 percent of girls from these military families said they had been in fights, compared to 28 percent of boys.

New Research Contradicts Old Assumptions

Nevertheless, experts say the findings contradict the traditional view that girls under stress exhibit "internalizing" behaviors, like becoming depressed or thinking about suicide, while boys are the ones who "externalize" through violent behavior

The new research may be something of a wake-up call for health professionals who deal with military families, one expert suggested.

"Maybe if we make assumptions about children, we may overlook other ways they may be suffering," said Dr. Gregory Gorman, an assistant professor of pediatrics at the Uniformed Services University of the Health Sciences in Bethesda, Md.

Additional research is needed to confirm the findings, said Reed, who has since left the University of Washington and is now a social worker with the Dana-Farber Cancer Institute in Boston [Massachusetts]. For example, the survey found that 10 to 20 percent of the adolescents in deployed families said they were in gangs. That's surprisingly high—more like something seen in New York City in the 1950s. Perhaps a larger, more national study would produce a lower number.

But it's not surprising that kids in deployed families would seek out other kids to help them deal with stress, said Gregory Leskin, a UCLA [University of California Los Angeles] psychologist who is director of a military family program at the National Child Traumatic Stress Network.

"Adolescents maybe able to get lost in social networks," he said.

Children in Military Families Are More Self-Sufficient and Responsible than Their Peers

Michael Clawson

Michael Clawson is an attorney who practices law in Colorado Springs, Colorado.

Military brats unite! As crazy as life seems for the military parent—moving all over the world, switching schools and making new friends—to the military child it can be one of life's greatest adventures. But some would argue that the mobile lifestyle of a military family is not as glamorous as it sounds.

When one or both parents are deployed in another part of the world, it can be an incredible stressor on children. Not only are they missing their parent; they also have new responsibilities at home and the added worries about their parent's safety. Kids may be resilient, but they may experience some difficulties in school with so much stress on the home front. One thing is for certain; military "brats" stick together and they make friends quickly. Military families lean heavily upon one another for strength and support because they never know when they'll have to pick up and move to another base.

From the outside, it may seem as if military kids have it made. They are far more patriotic and responsible than their non-military peers and they adapt faster to new situations and cultures. As a group they tend to be less materialistic and more adventurous, but there are also many disadvantages to this lifestyle. Let's take a look at the pros and cons of "growing up military."

The Pros

Foremost among a list of pros would be the enormous exposure that these kids get to other cultures, traditions, languages and cuisines. They are less attached to the typical American's way of life and quickly become well-rounded. Grown-up military brats say the experience they had as children added to their perspective and broadened their way of thinking. It also shaped their personalities because they had so many rich experiences with people from other parts of the world.

The early maturity shown by these kids is almost stunning when compared with their non-military peers.

Socially, military kids are very well adjusted. They get to meet so many interesting people from different countries, states and nationalities. Their friends are usually much more diverse than kids who live in civilian communities, and they learn how to talk to anyone about anything. These days, with the rise of social media and texting, military kids can stay in touch easier than ever before. As a result, distances no longer pose any restrictions to maintaining friends from all over the world.

Last, but certainly not least on the list of pros, is the military brat's self-sufficiency and how they learn to take care of themselves early in life. Kids whose parents are in the military may learn how to handle small tasks instead of being coddled. They are all too familiar with being dropped off at a new school and going in with the confidence that they will make new friends quickly. As a result, the early maturity shown by these kids is almost stunning when compared with their non-military peers.

Just the knowledge that one of their parents is out there fighting for their country and may not come home and the reality that they may need to look out for younger siblings helps them become more appreciative and respectful. They also develop a form of patriotism and deference to authority that cannot be taught in school.

The Cons

One of the hardest questions a military brat would have to answer is "Where are you from?" The truth is, military families have a rootless existence that can cause confusion among children resulting in an identity crisis of some kind. Frequent moves may not impact the extroverted child who adapts well to new situations; however the introverted kid could resent the military lifestyle. It may seem like as soon as they get settled somewhere they have to start all over again somewhere else. They may be able to list all the places they've lived, but there is hardly a place that they could call "home."

Long separations from one parent can be hard enough when a service member is deployed, but sometimes the entire family cannot move to a new location at the same time. This occurs when kids enter their important high school years and the family decides not to make the move until after graduation. Teens can find themselves depressed for a little while until they become accustomed to their parent's absence or the whole family is reunited.

Every military family has a different story to tell about how the lifestyle has affected their family life, and each military brat has a unique experience growing up in this fashion, but most have so many cherished memories that they wouldn't trade places with their civilian counterparts.

Military Children Are Resilient but Still Face Challenges

Patty Barron

Patty Barron is the director of family programs for the Association of the United States Army, a private nonprofit organization that supports the Army.

In order to truly support our military children, especially in today's military environment, it is important we understand who military kids are, what current challenges they face, and where their strength and resilience comes from.

According to the Department of Defense 2009 Demographics Report, there are approximately 2 million children of active and reserve component forces combined. Of these children, over 42 percent are five or below.

In addition, children 10 years of age or below have not ever, in their lifetimes, been in a world without war.

Several studies have pointed to the fact that our military children, although very adaptable, have been affected by the cumulative effects of stress and separations from their service member parent.

A study conducted by Patricia Lester, M.D., et al, titled "The Long War and Parental Combat Deployment: Effects on Military Children and At-Home Spouses" found that children affected by parental combat deployments showed considerable resilience compared to civilian children on several psychological health measures.

However, about one-third of the children reported clinically significant anxiety symptoms on standardized assessment. The study also showed that greater months of deployment separation and greater parental distress were risk factors for child emotional and behavioral problems.

A similar study conducted by the RAND Corporation, "Views from the Homefront," also found challenges related to how children and spouses handled new household responsibilities, how children deal with the stress of parental deployment and reintegration, and how families addressed changes in parent-child and family relationships.

Military children are resilient. . . . Studies show that approximately two thirds of children in military families are coping well.

The study identified a few groups that reported the most challenges: (1) spouses who had more emotional difficulties, (2) families experiencing more months of deployment, (3) older teens, (4) girls in dealing with the period of time when the deployed parent returns home, and (5) reserve component families.

The study also showed that families with good communication between parents and kids were able to weather the stress of deployment better.

These studies have helped us to quantify what we have always known anecdotally. Children do best when their parents are doing well emotionally; cumulative months of separation can take their toll, and symptoms of anxiety among some military children can persists even after the deployed service member has returned.

However, military children are resilient. Both studies show that approximately two thirds of children in military families are coping well.

What makes a military child so special? Why, in the face of so much adversity, do they manage to continue to thrive?

Great answers come from the kids themselves. In "Ten Things Military Kids Want You to Know," a publication of the

National Military Family Association, thousands of kids who attended the association's "Operation Purple" ® camps were asked to name the best and most challenging aspects of a military life.

Without missing a beat the kids' top three answers were pride, service, and community.

Pride, that comes from having a parent in the military serving their country. "I hope one day to be as great as him." Service because kids felt very strongly that they serve too, and community, because most military children live outside the gates in civilian neighborhoods and according to the toolkit: "They look within their community for friendship and support, especially during long deployments."

Support for our children must come from many directions. We have seen a plethora of programs and initiatives created to support military children. All the way from Sesame Street to the White House, the message is loud and clear, we are proud of you.

The first lady's appearance on the "iCarly" show just to say "thank you for your service," Elmo and his dad singing "Proud" on Sesame Workshop's popular "Talk, Listen, Connect DVD Series," and the public service announcements aimed at military families starring Tom Hanks, Oprah Winfrey and Steven Spielberg show that community support is there and growing.

The Army too has done its part. For those children that struggle with behavioral health issues the Army surgeon general in 2010 established the Child, Adolescent and Family Behavioral Health Office.

Its mission is to serve as the Army surgeon general's lead for developing, implementing and sustaining programs that achieve a behavioral health (BH) system of care promoting healthy, strong children and families.

The CAF-BHO is the proponent for two key programs focused on the BH needs of children and families, the Child and Family Assistance Center (CAFAC) and the School Behavioral Health (SBH) service.

The CAFAC's goal is to consolidate existing family-based behavioral health departments and augment their capability to care for children and families through integration and coordination of these services and increasing the number of providers based on the needs of the installation.

An example of how this has been done at Joint Base Lewis-McChord is described in the www.Army.mil July 13, 2010, article titled "Army Families Now Have a One-Stop Shop for Behavioral Health Services."

At JBLM, the Family Assistance for Maintaining Excellence, the Child Guidance Clinic and the School-Based Behavioral Health Program have been absorbed into the CAFAC.

Madigan Army Medical Center now has a fully-functioning one-stop shop under one director.

The CAFAC also provides one phone number that puts family members at JBLM in touch with providers who can deliver the care they need.

The transitional life that military kids live is also a life full of new experiences and opportunity.

The SBH offers access to behavioral health providers trained in child psychology, psychiatry and social work case management.

Teams of these providers are actually embedded in the schools that military children attend and work in conjunction with other specialists who are working on behalf of the wellness and behavioral health needs of Army children.

Currently, SBH programs have been established at over 40 schools at seven installations. These programs are only operating at on-post schools, but planning is underway to take the program to schools "outside the gate."

It has been said that military children are our nations' children.

The transitional life that military kids live is also a life full of new experiences and opportunity. It is our job to ensure that as much as possible, those experiences are good ones.

Adolescents in Military Families Generally Cope Well with the Stress of Parental Deployment

Leonard Wong and Stephen Gerras

Leonard Wong is a research professor in the Strategic Studies Institute at the US Army War College. Stephen Gerras is a professor of behavioral sciences in the Department of Command, Leadership, and Management at the US Army War College.

We have explored factors that may be associated with the stress experienced by a child while his or her parent is deployed. A related but somewhat broader question asks how an adolescent copes with a life of deployments. Beyond identifying methods that may alleviate stress during a single deployment, we attempted to isolate factors that strongly predict how well Army adolescents handle multiple deployments overall. This inquiry moved away from a focus on day-to-day stresses and instead examined strategies for dealing with the difficult role of a son or daughter of a soldier during a long war.

Before attempting to identify the various factors that may be associated with the ability of adolescents to cope with deployments, we compiled a baseline assessment based on previous research. . . . According to spouse responses in the 2005 Survey of Army Families, 49 percent of the adolescents were coping well or very well with deployments. The 2008 DoD [Department of Defense] Spouse survey showed nearly identical results. The spouse perspective in the current 2009 study also shows almost identical results—which at first appears un-

Leonard Wong and Stephen Gerras, *The Effects of Multiple Deployments on Army Adolescents*, U.S. Army War College Strategic Studies Institute, January 2010. Reproduced by permission.

remarkable, but the similarities in the spouse responses reinforce the representativeness of the sample in the current study.

The findings illustrate an unanticipated and remarkable resiliency in most Army adolescents in dealing with lives marked by multiple deployments.

However, shifting to the soldier perspective introduces an interesting finding. Soldiers appear to be more pessimistic with estimates that a third of their children are coping poorly or very poorly with deployments. A possible explanation for the pessimism of soldiers could be that they feel responsible for subjecting their families to deployment separations in the first place and therefore tend to heighten negative perceptions because of guilt. Soldiers may also be less apt to believe that, despite their repeated absences, their children can fare well without them.

From the adolescent perspective, the contrast is even greater, yet in the opposite direction. When asked how they handled deployments overall, a surprising 56 percent of Army adolescents responded that they coped well or very well, while a much lower 17 percent said they coped poorly or very poorly. In other words, adolescents are significantly more optimistic about their overall ability to handle deployments than either spouses or soldiers.

Before celebrating the unexpectedly high percentage of adolescents who claimed they handled deployments well, we must remember that the results can be extrapolated to imply that over 20,000 adolescent children in active duty Army families alone are not coping well with deployments. Soldiers have long known that wars inevitably result in casualties. To believe otherwise would be naive and foolhardy. Today's Army adolescents realize that they too are inextricably linked to the warfight, and that they too will suffer casualties. If one out of every six Army adolescents reports doing poorly with repeated deployments, the situation can hardly be considered acceptable. Yet, the findings illustrate an unanticipated and remarkable resiliency in most Army adolescents in dealing with lives marked by multiple deployments.

Increased ability to cope with a life of deployments tended to be associated with higher participation in religious . . . activities.

Factors in Ability to Handle Deployments

What factors best determine an adolescent's overall ability to handle deployments? We analyzed the relationship between an adolescent's coping ability and the original six factors—multiple deployments, a strong family, supportive mentors, activities, communication, and personal beliefs. As expected, the strength of the family had a significant influence on an adolescent's ability to cope with deployments. [The study] shows the tendency of children whose soldier parents assessed their families as strong to report a better ability to cope with deployments. To minimize single-rater bias, we again assessed family strength from the soldier's perspective. . . .

To eliminate bias coming from a single perspective, the assessment of the spouse's reaction came from the spouse while the assessment of the child's ability to handle deployments was provided by the adolescent. For many children, a key factor in how well they cope with deployments is the at-home parent's handling of the deployment. For example, when asked what enables him to deal with deployments, the 13-year-old son of a specialist attributed it to, "My mom . . . for everything she has gone through since my dad left. She has stayed strong for us." A sergeant's 14-year-old daughter was a bit more to the point when she ascribed her ability to cope with his absence to "the other parent not acting like a drama queen."

While adolescent involvement in sports or clubs was correlated with lower stress during a deployment, these same activities were not associated with higher levels of adolescent coping ability. Instead, increased ability to cope with a life of deployments tended to be associated with higher participation in religious (chapel, church, or place of worship) activities. Similarly, survey results also showed that those children involved in youth organizations such as Boy Scouts or Girl Scouts reported higher overall ability to handle a long period of repeated deployments.

The best predictor of a child's overall ability to cope with deployments is their belief that deployed soldiers make a difference.

These findings may reflect how different types of activities might relate to different outcomes. For activities that require daily attendance and focus—like sports teams, band practice, or play rehearsals—the main effect may be a diversion from thinking about the negative aspects of a deployment. Thus, participation in these types of activities coincides with lower levels of stress during a deployment.

Participation in church or chapel activities and involvement in organizations such as Scouting, on the other hand, may provide less frequent distractions and are therefore not related to deployment stress. Participation in religious activities and Scouting, though, may work in a more abstract manner as adolescents' thoughts are redirected to spiritual or service-oriented concepts such as selflessness and sacrifice. Involvement in such activities, while not significantly related to the stress of a single deployment, may help adolescents to cope more broadly with a life of repeated deployments. . . . The magnitude of the effect is not as large as factors involving the strength of the family or spousal reaction to a deployment, but the trend is still significant.

The Importance of Believing That Soldiers Make a Difference

Earlier, we established that adolescent attitudes, such as the perception of America's support for the war, could significantly influence perceptions of deployment stress. The degree to which adolescents believe American society supports the war also significantly relates to their overall ability to cope with deployments. A surprising finding concerning the attitudes of adolescents, however, was the strength of the relationship between their ability to cope with deployments and their belief that deployed soldiers are making a difference in the world. . . . The greater their belief that deployed soldiers are making a difference, the more likely adolescents are to report that they are coping well with a life of deployments. While that belief may not be a significant predictor of the stress experienced during an individual deployment, it is strongly related to their ability to better cope with multiple deployments.

We must applaud this generation of children—often questioned for its lack of resolve—for answering uncertainty with patience, hardship with perseverance, and difficulty with resilience.

Surprisingly, multivariate analysis shows that the best predictor of a child's overall ability to cope with deployments is their belief that deployed soldiers make a difference. In order, the next best predictors of an adolescent's ability to cope are a strong family, followed by the child's belief that America supports the war, then a strong nondeployed spouse. A finding that the strength of a child's family is strongly related to his or her ability to cope with deployments is predictable. But it is neither obvious nor expected that the best predictor of an Army adolescent's ability to cope with multiple deployments would be their conviction that, deployed soldiers are making a difference.

And yet, the finding is very intuitive. Army adolescents grow up in an environment laden with lofty notions such as sacrifice, duty, and selfless service. They are accustomed to hearing common Army aphorisms such as "I know my soldiers and I will always place their needs above my own," and "I will always place the mission first." They understand that the Army is a "greedy" institution that demands all of their parent's time, energy, and focus. They also understand from firsthand experience that the family is another greedy institution requiring constant attention and care. They see deployed soldiers caught in the middle—struggling to maintain balance in the pull of both noble institutions.

Some Army adolescents contend poorly in this dilemma; others—many more than soldiers or Army spouses would indicate—say they are doing amazingly well in these trying times. They still suffer from stress and anxiety during each deployment, but they can handle the life of an Army adolescent if they remain confident that the repeated absences of their parent are not in vain. The maturity of today's Army adolescents is exemplified by the comments of the very discerning 16-year-old daughter of a sergeant major who stated:

> My daddy always being gone makes me stress out the most. He is in charge of a lot of soldiers and he always has to do what they do. "Set the example," he says, "Don't ask a soldier to do something you can't or won't do." I get scared that sometimes he will forget to be careful and he will get hurt. He has deployed so many times already, but he tells me to not worry. "Somebody has to do the job and take care of the younger soldiers."

> I just wish that sometimes he would forget about soldiers and remember me and my sisters. We need him too. I just wish the fighting would stop, then he would be able to stay home with us. I love my daddy to death, but he will never give up on taking care of his soldiers.

Despite the findings of this monograph, there are still many unknowns concerning the effects of deployments. We cannot predict how these children will negotiate the often difficult transition to adulthood. Nor do we know how an adolescence spent in the turbulence of a deployed Army will affect these young people when they eventually become parents. But we must applaud this generation of children—often questioned for its lack of resolve—for answering uncertainty with patience, hardship with perseverance, and difficulty with resilience.

There Are Many Reasons to Admire Military Kids

Elaine Sanchez

Elaine Sanchez is a writer for Brooke Army Medical Center Public Affairs.

In honor of April's Month of the Military Child [2013], I created a Top 10 list of the qualities I most appreciate about children from military families. Their amazing service and sacrifice deserve a much longer list, but I figured this would at least be a start.

The top 10 reasons I appreciate military children:

10. Their sense of humor. Military kids do all they can to keep their spirits up. Some carry life-sized cardboard posters of parents called "Flat Daddies" and "Flat Mommies" to keep deployed loved ones close at hand. They carry them to pizza parties and movies, sporting events and concerts. During a past deployment, military wife Vivian Greentree's sons took it a step further. They pasted pictures of their deployed dad on a stick, dubbed it a "dad on a stick" and took it everywhere with them. They even asked their "dad" to help them make macaroni and cheese.

9. They selflessly serve their community. Military children possess a strong sense of service—perhaps modeled after their military parents who serve and sacrifice daily. A shining example is last year's Army Military Child of the Year, Amelia McConnell. Soon after her father returned from Iraq in 2006, he was diagnosed with leukemia. After treatment, he redeployed to Iraq in 2007. In 2009, her only brother, Sgt. Andrew McConnell, was killed in Afghanistan. Still, Amelia excelled in school and in sports, and volunteered hundreds of hours a

Elaine Sanchez, "Top 10 Reasons I Admire Military Kids," Department of Defense, April 2013.

year for a number of organizations. When asked why she does so much she said, "I always think there are a lot of people in worse situations than I am."

8. They stand by their military parent through thick and thin. I met a high school senior several years ago who told me his father would miss his graduation and his departure to college. But this teen wasn't upset in the least. "He loves to be a soldier, and if it makes him happy, it makes me happy," he said. "How can I possibly complain that he's not watching me graduate when he's out there sacrificing for our nation."

7. Their sense of patriotism. Zachary Laychak was 9 years old when his father was killed on Sept. 11, 2001, when American Airlines Flight 77 crashed into the Pentagon. Laychak struggled over the years with anger and confusion over the incident. But as time passed, his initial anger evolved into a deep sense of patriotism. "As terrible as this whole situation was, I know he was a very patriotic person," he said of his father, "and that he died serving his country. That's a way he would have been proud to go."

Military kids ... have an innate appreciation for cultural diversity and knowledge of world events that most kids who never crossed state lines would be hard-pressed to match.

Military Kids Support Each Other

6. They support each other. Several years ago, I met an amazing group of military kids at a camp for children of fallen service members hosted by the Tragedy Assistance Program for Survivors. Over the course of a long weekend in [Washington,] D.C., the children bonded over their shared experiences, offering hope and support to each other. The camp and fellow survivors give "us a sense of we're not alone in this fight of grieving," said attendee, Ben Suplee, whose father, Sgt. 1st Class Daniel A. Suplee, died while serving in Afghanistan.

5. Their adaptability. Military children change school systems six to nine times on average. Felicity and Abigail Horan, twin daughters of Army Lt. Col. Dave Horan, described their experiences as military kids at a "Joining Forces" event last year. Now in the seventh grade, the girls are attending their fifth school after eight military moves. They spoke of "always saying goodbye" to friends and that their father missed five of their birthdays. But, Felicity said, "Don't feel sorry for us. . . . We are stronger because of our experiences."

4. Their compassion. A number of kids have military parents who return home wounded, some with visible wounds and others with less-evident injuries such as post-traumatic stress disorder or traumatic brain injury. These kids immediately step up to help out at home—taking on additional chores, pitching in to babysit—during their parent's recovery. Army Spc. Kevin Wear, father of five, suffered a traumatic brain injury and leg injury in Afghanistan when a roadside bomb blew up the vehicle he was riding in. He often struggles to remember dates and words, but his kids don't see him any differently. "All five of my kids believe I'm Superman—the toughest, strongest guy in the world," he said.

3. Their global knowledge. Many military kids have traveled across the nation and around the world. They have an innate appreciation for cultural diversity and knowledge of world events that most kids who never crossed state lines would be hard-pressed to match. At a Joining Forces event last year, Army Chief of Staff Gen. Raymond T. Odierno said he understands the challenges faced by military families—he moved his wife and children 24 times during his 36-year military career. Today, the general said, his children are successful adults in large part because of their military upbringing, the resilience it adds, and the teachers who took an interest in them.

Military Kids Meet Challenges

2. Their strength. They've dealt with a decade of war and multiple deployments, with the associated worry and fear. But these challenges also have equipped them with a resilience that will prepare them for life's setbacks and hardships. Nicole Marie Daly, the Army's 2013 Child of the Year, has moved nine times and has attended three high schools so far. Growing up in a military family "created resiliency because every time we move, I have to constantly prove myself as an individual and my capabilities," Nicole said.

1. They serve too. Their military parent signed on the dotted line; their children did not. Yet, they must deal with deployments, frequent moves and school transitions, and they do so with courage and grace. As a nation, we owe them a debt of gratitude, First Lady Michelle Obama told a group of high school girls last April [2012]. "Ultimately, you understand that your parents are part of something far bigger than themselves," she said. "By working so hard . . . , you give your parents the peace of mind they need to focus on their mission. With your service, you make their service possible. And for that, we can't thank you enough."

CHAPTER 4

What Is the Government Doing to Help Military Families?

Overview: The First Lady Urges Americans to Support Military Families

Michelle Obama

Michelle Obama is the First Lady of the United States. She is married to President Barack Obama.

Last weekend [September 2011], Americans across the country joined together to remember that September morning from 10 years ago [September 11, 2001], honoring the memory of those we lost with service and reflection. And my husband [President Barack Obama] and I were humbled to stand with the families and survivors on the same hallowed grounds where tragedy struck.

Yet what shines most brightly from last weekend is not memories of horror, but images of heroes; not the echoes of evil that sought to divide, but the compassion that compelled us to unite. What lasts from this anniversary is the true spirit of America that was laid bare that day and remains alive today: the courage of those who lost loved ones; the strength of those who survived; the bravery of those who ran not away from but into danger.

Those are the same qualities that live on every day among a generation of American troops and their families whose service has been defined by 9/11 and its aftermath. This anniversary also gives us the opportunity to reflect on all that these families have endured and our obligations to them now and in the years ahead.

Selfless Service

They're the 9/11 Generation—the more than 5 million servicemembers who have worn the uniform this past decade

Michelle Obama, "Support Our Military Families," *White House Blog*, September 14, 2011.

and their families. They've rightfully earned not only the admiration of a grateful nation, but also a place in history alongside our greatest generations. More than 2 million men and women have served in the war zones, including an unprecedented number of deployments by our National Guardsmen and Reservists. We've never asked so much of our all-volunteer force.

Our military families always stand ready to serve their loved ones, their communities and our country.

And we've never asked this much of our military families, either. Found in nearly every community in this country, these brave family members serve right alongside their loved ones. They just don't wear uniforms. They're spouses who balance a career and a household all alone while their loved ones are deployed. They're young children who have known only life in a nation at war. They're teenagers who are all too familiar with Dad or Mom being gone for months at a time.

Yet even with all that they shoulder, these military family members are some of the most extraordinary individuals I've ever met: the moms who always seem to pick up the extra carpool shift, the kids who take on extra chores around the house, the survivors of our fallen who step up every day to serve our communities, and the veterans and wounded warriors who have served our country heroically on the battlefield and continue to contribute here at home.

It's Our Turn

No matter what the situation or how many directions they're being pulled in, our military families always stand ready to serve their loved ones, their communities and our country.

After 10 years of war, it's our turn to return their service and sacrifice with honor and appreciation of our own—and not just in word, but in deed.

That's why last spring, Jill Biden [Vice President Joe Biden's wife] and I launched Joining Forces, a national initiative to address the unique needs and expand the opportunities of these remarkable men, women and children. Businesses can work to employ veterans and help military spouses build careers. Schools can make sure they're properly supporting military kids. Citizens can reach out to organizations who serve military families right in their communities. Every single person, group or community can do something, and we've already seen countless individuals, organizations and businesses step up to answer this call. To see what others are up to, and to join forces yourself, please visit us at www.joiningforces .gov.

I hope you do.

As we reaffirm our commitment to hold dear the heroism, strength and compassion we saw on Sept. 11, let's also pledge to keep our military families in our hearts long after this anniversary has passed. These men, women and children have served valiantly in the decade since that fateful day.

Now it's up to us to serve them as well.

The Federal Government Has Specific Plans for Strengthening Military Families

Office of the US President

This is the introduction to an official government report, issued by the White House, that was prepared by representatives from the staffs of all the Cabinet Secretaries.

The President [Barack Obama] has made the care and support of military families a top national security policy priority. We recognize that military families come from the active duty Armed Forces, the National Guard, and the Reserves. They support and sustain troops fighting to defend the Nation, they care for our wounded warriors, and they survive our fallen heroes. The well-being of military families is an important indicator of the well-being of the overall force. At a time when America is at war and placing considerable, sustained demands on its troops and their families, it is especially important to address the family, home, and community challenges facing our all-volunteer force. For years to come, military families and Veterans will continue to face unique challenges, and at the same time will also have great potential to continue contributing to our communities and country.

Less than 1 percent of Americans serve in uniform today, but they bear 100 percent of the burden of defending our Nation. Currently, more than 2.2 million service members make up America's all-volunteer force in the active, National Guard, and Reserve components. Since September 11, 2001, more than two million troops have been deployed to Iraq and Af-

Office of the United States President, *Strengthening Our Military Families: Meeting America's Commitment*, The White House, January 2011.

ghanistan. Fifty five percent of the force is married and 40 percent have two children. Only 37 percent of our families live on military installations; the remaining 63 percent live in over 4,000 communities nationwide. Multiple deployments, combat injuries, and the challenges of reintegration can have far-reaching effects on not only the troops and their families, but also upon America's communities as well. These challenges should be at the forefront of our national discourse.

In May 2010, the President directed the National Security Staff (NSS) to develop a coordinated Federal Government-wide approach to supporting military families. By harnessing resources and expertise across the Federal Government, the Obama Administration is improving the quality of military family life, helping communities more effectively support military families, and thereby improving the long-term effectiveness of U.S. military forces. Our vision is to ensure that:

- the U.S. military recruits and retains the highest-caliber volunteers to contribute to the Nation's defense and security;

- Service members can have strong family lives while maintaining the highest state of readiness;

- civilian family members can live fulfilling lives while supporting their service member(s); and

- the United States better understands and appreciates the experience, strength, and commitment to service of our military families.

This report was prepared by an Interagency Policy Committee (IPC) involving representatives from the staffs of all Cabinet Secretaries, with oversight from the NSS and Domestic Policy Council (DPC), and in response to Presidential Study Directive/PSD-9.

With the involvement of the National Economic Council, Office of the First Lady [Michelle Obama], and the Office of

Dr. [Jill] Biden [wife of Vice President Joe Biden], the IPC has identified four priority areas to address the concerns and challenges of the families of Active Duty and Reserve Component Army, Navy, Air Force, Marines, and Coast Guard members; Veterans; and those who have fallen. While the Coast Guard is a component with the Department of Homeland Security, for the purposes of this report, it should be assumed to be included in the initiatives supporting all military families, as applicable. This government-wide effort will:

1. Enhance the well-being and psychological health of the military family,

    1.1. By increasing behavioral health care services through prevention-based alternatives and integrating community-based services;

    1.2. By building awareness among military families and communities that psychological fitness is as important as physical fitness;

    1.3. By protecting military members and families from unfair financial practices and helping families enhance their financial readiness;

    1.4. By eliminating homelessness and promoting home security among Veterans and military families;

    1.5. By ensuring availability of critical substance abuse prevention, treatment, and recovery services for Veterans and military families; and

    1.6. By making our court systems more responsive to the unique needs of Veterans and families.

2. Ensure excellence in military children's education and their development,

    2.1. By improving the quality of the educational experience;

    2.2. By reducing negative impacts of frequent relocations and absences; and

    2.3. By encouraging the healthy development of military children.

3. Develop career and educational opportunities for military spouses,

    3.1. By increasing opportunities for Federal careers;

    3.2. By increasing opportunities for private-sector careers;

    3.3. By increasing access to educational advancement;

    3.4. By reducing barriers to employment and services due to different State policies and standards; and

    3.5. By protecting the rights of service members and families.

4. Increase child care availability and quality for the Armed Forces,

    4.1. By enhancing child care resources within the Department of Defense and the Coast Guard.

This is an enduring effort. Each Cabinet secretary has pledged his or her individual commitment to this important task. Together as a team, we are committed to implementing our plans, assessing our results on a recurring basis with continued transparency, seeking constant feedback, and ensuring the Federal Government has the capacity to support and engage military families throughout their lives.

The Federal Consumer Financial Protection Bureau Helps Military Families with Problems

Holly Petraeus

Holly Petraeus is an assistant director of the Consumer Financial Protection Bureau who heads its Office of Servicemember Affairs. She is the mother, sister, daughter, granddaughter, great-granddaughter, and spouse of servicemembers.

During my travels to military installations across the United States I have talked with servicemembers and their families from coast to coast, and some of the issues I mentioned in my last testimony here [before the Senate Committee on Banking, Housing and Urban Affairs] continue to be hot-button items. First and foremost are the financial concerns of military homeowners. As I'm sure you know, some of the states that have the largest concentration of military bases are also the ones that were very hard hit during the housing downturn. In almost every town hall or roundtable I conduct, housing concerns are a major topic of conversation. In particular, active-duty servicemembers who own homes and have seen them drop in value and go "underwater" are faced with a true dilemma when they receive Permanent Change of Station (PCS) orders and have to move. What do they do with a house they can't sell for enough to pay it off? PCS orders come with a short timeline, and military homeowners have not been getting the assistance they need, either in programs tailored to their unique circumstances or in timely information about foreclosure alternatives.

Holly Petraeus, Testimony before the Senate Committee on Banking, United States Senate, June 26, 2012.

Both at town halls and through the [Consumer Financial Protection Bureau] CFPB's complaint system we've heard from military homeowners that they have been:

- Told there was no help available;

- Told they had to be delinquent on their mortgage before they could qualify for help, and even advised to skip payments;

- Asked to waive their rights under the Servicemembers Civil Relief Act (SCRA) in order to be evaluated for assistance;

- Stalled with repeated demands for loan documents that have already been sent;

- Routed to a different loan-servicing official with each call;

- Denied the interest-rate reduction or foreclosure protection required by the SCRA;

- Listed as "failing to respond" while deployed despite the fact that their spouse had a power of attorney and was providing the requested information to the servicer;

- And given information about foreclosure alternatives too late to do any good.

In recent years a number of servicemembers have seen no viable alternative but to leave their family in their "underwater" house and go alone to their new duty station.

Help for Military Homeowners

I've been talking about these issues with a number of parties and I'm pleased to report that progress has been made for military homeowners. First of all, a recent settlement between the federal government, 49 states and the District of Columbia and the five largest mortgage servicers (Citigroup, JP Morgan Chase, Wells Fargo, Bank of America and Ally Financial) addressed some of the SCRA issues—mandating look-backs and compensation by the servicers where they had denied SCRA benefits—and provided some short-sale opportunities and deficiency waivers for servicemembers with PCS orders. Also, the government-sponsored enterprises, Fannie Mae [the Federal National Mortgage Association (FNMA)] and Freddie Mac [Federal Home Loan Mortgage Corporation], have both published guidance to servicers that says that a military PCS move is a qualifying hardship for loan-modification or other assistance.

And last week [June 2012] the Federal Housing Finance Authority, which regulates Fannie Mae and Freddie Mac, not only announced that PCS orders are a qualifying hardship for a short sale, but also released guidance that a servicemember with a Fannie or Freddie loan will not be asked to make a financial contribution to receive the short sale, or be liable for the difference between the short sale amount and the original mortgage amount.

Further, I was able to work with the Department of the Treasury—specifically, the Assistant Secretary for Financial Stability, Tim Massad—to encourage changes to the Home Affordable Modification Program (HAMP) guidelines that will provide more opportunities for mortgage assistance to military homeowners. As of June 1st [2012] military homeowners who have to move because of PCS orders, but intend to come back to their house and do not buy another house elsewhere, can still qualify as "owner-occupants," making them eligible for a HAMP Tier 1 mortgage loan modification. I was really pleased to see this change in the guidance because military personnel have been effectively cut off from so much foreclosure-prevention assistance due to requirements that the home be "owner-occupied." That's just not possible for a servicemember on orders. My husband and I are a case in point, as we moved 24 times in 37 years and I have never lived in a house more than 4 years straight, and that only once. In recent years a number of servicemembers have seen no viable alternative but to leave their family in their "underwater" house and go alone to their new duty station, which may mean a separation of 3 years or more. I am hopeful this new guidance will help change that.

CFPB's Office of Students, through its "Know Before You Owe" project, has done a lot of work to ensure that prospective students can determine the cost of their college degree in advance.

The CFPB is continuing to take action to protect military homeowners. Last week, the CFPB, along with the prudential regulators—the Board of Governors of the Federal Reserve System, the Federal Deposit Insurance Corporation, the National Credit Union Administration and the Office of the Comptroller of the Currency—issued supervisory guidance for mortgage servicers specifically addressing the issues of military homeowners with PCS orders. The guidance not only reminds servicers of the need to provide important information in a timely manner, but also makes it clear that military homeowners with PCS orders should get accurate and clear information from their mortgage servicers early enough to make informed decisions that will minimize damage to their financial readiness.

Help for College Students

Now, to go on to another issue that has been a frequent topic of conversation since I last spoke before you: you may recall that I testified last November about aggressive marketing to military personnel and their families by certain institutions of higher education—pushing not only their educational programs, but also, in many cases, expensive private student loans to pay for the amount of tuition and fees not covered by military GI Bill or Tuition Assistance benefits. There is an extra incentive for for-profit colleges, in particular, to chase after military students because of the 90–10 proprietary college federal funding cap—a requirement that for-profit colleges get at least 10 percent of their revenue from sources other than Title IV federal education funds administered by the Department of Education. Military GI Bill and Tuition Assistance benefits are not considered Title IV funds, so they fall into the 10 percent category that these colleges need to fill. Some of your colleagues have recently submitted proposed legislation on this topic, and, in addition, a bipartisan group of more than 20 state Attorneys General recently wrote to Congress urging the moving of military education benefits to the 90 percent side of the 90–10 rule.

Basic Training is not a good place to absorb financial content, because recruits are tired, stressed and worried about their next meal and their next formation.

For our part, CFPB's Office of Students, through its "Know Before You Owe" project, has done a lot of work to ensure that prospective students can determine the cost of their college degree in advance and can compare financial-aid offers from various institutions. They developed a "financial aid shopping sheet" and posted a beta version on our website, ConsumerFinance.gov, encouraging visitors to give us suggestions on how to improve it. And students can also find on our website a Student Debt Repayment Assistant that can help them learn about their options when repaying their education loans.

On the same topic, on April 27th [2012] I was honored to accompany the President and the First Lady to Fort Stewart, Georgia to watch the President sign an Executive Order establishing principles of excellence for educational institutions serving military personnel, veterans, and their families. The Order directed the Departments of Defense, Veterans Affairs, and Education, in consultation with the CFPB and the Attorney General, to take steps to ensure that servicemembers, veterans and their families can get the information they need about the schools where they spend their education benefits. The Order also strengthens oversight and accountability within the federal military and veterans' educational benefits programs. And the CFPB is currently working with groups from the above agencies to see that the Order is implemented in a way that best serves our military and veterans.

Financial Education for Servicemembers

Another part of my job, as described in the Dodd-Frank Wall Street Reform and Consumer Protection Act (Dodd-Frank), is to "educate and empower service members and their families to make better informed decisions regarding consumer financial products and services." When I last appeared before you, I was in the process of taking a look at the financial education given to servicemembers at the front end of their career: at Basic Training and the Advanced School that follows it. A couple of things struck me as significant. First, that Basic Training is not a good place to absorb financial content, because recruits are tired, stressed and worried about their next meal and their next formation. And second, that recruits may already be in debt before they show up at Basic Training. I heard from staff at Lackland Air Force Base [Texas], which does Air Force Basic Training, that recruits arriving there in 2008 had an average of $10,000 in debt upon arrival.

Those two observations, among others, led us to a plan to provide a short financial-education curriculum that can be delivered via smartphone or computer during what the military calls the Delayed Entry Program (DEP). DEP comprises the period when an individual has committed to join the military, but has not yet arrived at boot camp, and DEP can range from two weeks to up to a year in length. It's a timeframe when a new recruit would have more time and less stress than at Basic Training so could focus on some "just-enough and just-in-time" financial lessons that could be very helpful before they get that first military paycheck and start thinking of ways to spend it. We feel that this curriculum will fill a niche where there is no financial education at present, and the Pentagon, including the Senior Enlisted members of all the services, is enthusiastic about the idea and has signaled its intent to help us field it.

Consumer Protection for Military Families and Veterans

Finally, I'd like to highlight a few of the consumer-protection issues that I've heard about repeatedly in recent months from military and veteran families and those who provide support services to them. Let me mention that I am also charged under Dodd-Frank with coordinating efforts among Federal and state agencies on consumer protection measures relating to consumer financial products and services offered to or used by servicemembers and their families.

The first issue is aggressive and deceptive tactics by debt collectors specifically targeting members of the military. These tactics have included:

- Contacting the servicemember's military chain of command as a way to coerce payment;

- Putting a clause in the loan contract that the servicemember must grant the debt collector the right to contact the chain of command;

- Threatening punishment under the Uniform Code of Military Justice, threatening to have the servicemember reduced in rank, or threatening to have the servicemember's security clearance revoked; and

- Contacting a spouse after deployment of the service-member and pressuring the spouse to repay right away without the benefit of communicating with the service-member, or, in one particularly appalling instance, demanding that the widow of a servicemember killed in combat pay them immediately from the combat death gratuity.

The second issue, and one that has been the subject of a hearing this month [June 2012] by the Senate Special Committee on Aging, concerns abuses connected with the veterans' benefit known as Aid and Attendance. This benefit is designed to provide assistance with basic daily activities such as cooking and bathing to severely disabled veterans who have very limited means, and the benefit can amount to two thousand dollars or more per month. I have heard from a number of state Veterans Affairs [VA] directors, starting with my trip to Montana in January, that they are concerned about the increasing number of individuals and companies that use Aid and Attendance as a hook to sell their services to elderly veterans.

The Internet is full of "military loans," some outright scams and others with very high interest rates.

Aid and Attendance offers can take a variety of forms:

- It may be an offer from a lawyer or "veterans' advisor" to get the Aid and Attendance benefit for you—for a fee. In reality there is free VA claims-processing assistance available in every state, accessible by contacting the state Department of Veterans Affairs.

- It may be a claim from a paid advisor that they can get the benefit for you more quickly than anyone else. But all VA benefits claims have to go through the standard VA evaluation process, and no one can bypass the system to get your claim approved faster than usual.

- It may involve helping you qualify for Aid and Attendance, if you have too much money, by taking control of your assets and moving them into a trust where you can't access them. This, in turn, may disqualify you for other assistance such as Medicaid, and it also means that you can't get at your money—whereas the scammer can.

- Also, some retirement homes are now using the lure of Aid and Attendance to get veterans to move in on the premise that they will get Aid and Attendance and it will pay for everything. In cases where the claim is denied after the veteran has already spent money to move in, this leaves the veteran in the untenable position of being unable to afford to remain in the facility.

The CFPB has an Office of Financial Protection for Older Americans and my office is working with them on this issue. They have a statutory requirement to give recommendations to Congress on the vetting of financial advisors for seniors and have included some questions about fraudulent or deceptive practices that target older veterans and/or military retirees in a recent Request for Information published in the *Federal Register*. We look forward to reading the responses and exploring ways in which we can be helpful on this issue.

Protection Against Loan Scams

One more consumer-protection area of concern continues to be installment loans marketed to the military. I hear from financial counselors on the installations about the prevalence of payday-like products that are specifically marketed to military families—often with patriotic-sounding names and the American flags on the website to match, but with a sky-high interest rate for the servicemember who takes out the loan. And the Internet is full of "military loans," some outright scams and others with very high interest rates.

Although the Military Lending Act put a 36 percent cap on the annual percentage rate of certain types of loans to the active-duty military, some lenders have found ways to get outside of the definitions in the Department of Defense (DoD) rule implementing the Military Lending Act. We know from our discussions with representatives from the DoD that they intend to revisit the Military Lending Act rule later this year, either in response to changes in the law or to see if the definitions in the rule need to be updated to reflect changes in lending practices since the initial release of the regulation.

Also, in May the Deputy Assistant Secretary of Defense for Military Community and Family Policy, Robert L. Gordon, III and I signed a Joint Statement of Principles on Small-Dollar Lending, and we at the CFPB look forward to working with the DoD on creating strong consumer protections for servicemembers in the small-dollar lending marketplace.

In conclusion, the Office of Servicemember Affairs is working hard to fulfill its mission to work on consumer financial education and consumer-protection measures for military personnel and their families. I think we've seen some promising developments since I last appeared before you, and we will press on to work on existing problems and also address new issues as they arise. Our military and their families have done extraordinary service for our country, and, in return, it's an honor for me and my staff to serve them through our work at the Office of Servicemember Affairs.

The Department of Defense Works to Ensure a Good Education for Military Children

Leon E. Panetta

Leon E. Panetta was the US Secretary of Defense from 2011 to 2013.

It is a distinct privilege for me to be able to come down to Texas and to be among so many who share a dedication to helping our military children have a better future, and that's what it's all about.

I feel a special relationship to this group, not just because I'm Secretary of Defense, but because I spent two years in the Army with my family and with my kids and I had the opportunity to see the great work that was done as just a trooper on the lines seeing exactly the services that were provided. And also, I had a sister-in-law who taught at one of the schools that I was at. So I've got a good sense of the dedication that's involved by all of you to try to make sure that our military kids get the best education possible.

I am pleased to be joined by the Chairman of the Joint Chiefs who also will be here, as well as a number of our Service Chiefs and I think that tells you a lot.

Their presence underscores the importance of education to military families and to the ability of our armed forces. And it does relate to this and we shouldn't lose sight of it. What you do relates to our ability to carry out the mission of defending the country.

Leon E. Panetta, "Military Children Education Coalition," Speech at Grapevine, Texas, Department of Defense, June 27, 2012.

We are all here—the Chiefs, those involved in military leadership—to say thank you. Thank you on behalf of the Department of Defense. I deeply appreciate all of the work that so many here and around the country are doing to help our military families.

In a democracy, we are dependent on good education. Education is the key to self-government, it's the key to opportunity, it's the key to equality, it's the key to freedom, it's the key to a better life.

As you know, I am the son of Italian immigrants who came to this country like millions of others seeking the opportunity that this country has to offer. They came with little money, few language abilities, few skills.

Helping to give future generations a better quality of life is what goes to the very heart of our military.

A Better Life for Children

My son—I've got three sons—my youngest son looked up the manifest for when my parents came through Ellis Island. And my parents are listed and my father's occupation was listed as "peasant." So he had to come to this country to work hard and to be a part of what America has to offer.

I used to ask my father "Why would you do that? Why would you travel all that distance, not knowing where the hell you were going, not having any idea, why would you do that?" And yes, they came from a poor area in Italy. But they also had the comfort of family. Why would you pick up and suddenly leave all of that to travel thousands of miles to come to a strange country? And my father said the reason was that my mother and he thought that they could give their children a better life.

And that's the American dream—that's what all of us want for our children and it's hopefully what they will want for

155

their children because that is the fundamental American dream, giving our kids a better life. It is what we want for our children and for this country.

And helping to give future generations a better quality of life is what goes to the very heart of our military, and what everybody here is doing. That is because giving our children a quality education is essential to giving them a better life.

I've long believed that this country has an obligation to make education a top national priority. I would not be here as Secretary of Defense were it not for the opportunities that were given to me by education. I have a lot to be thankful for—thankful to my parents who basically kicked my ass and said "You better get a good education," thankful to the nuns that taught me in Catholic grammar school who also incidentally kicked my ass, thankful to a lot of inspiring teachers at the public high school that I went to in Monterey [California], thankful to the Jesuits who taught me at the University of Santa Clara and who taught me that one of the fundamental purposes of education is to help our fellow human beings.

Educating military children is not only important to their future, it's also critically important to the future of our military and, indeed, to the future of our nation.

Over the course of my career, because of what education gave to me, I had the opportunity to be able to give back and to help strengthen the national commitment to education. I served as Director of the Office for Civil Rights at the old Department of Health, Education and Welfare, had the opportunity to work on efforts to promote equal education for all, served in Congress and as Budget Chair, worked on education budgets, did that as Director of the Office of Management and Budget, and ultimately as White House Chief of Staff to President [Bill] Clinton.

After I left government and went back home, my wife and I decided to establish an institute for public policy at California State University at Monterey Bay. It is an institute—and my wife continues to run that institute—dedicated to attracting the best young men and women to lives of public service, and to try to inspire them how important it is to give something back to this country, and to try to give them the tools and the knowledge they need in order to succeed in their careers.

Now, as Secretary of Defense, I am determined to do everything possible to give our military children the tools they need to succeed in the future.

The Importance of Education

Educating military children is not only important to *their* future, it's also critically important to the future of *our* military and, indeed, to the future of *our* nation.

When it comes to education there are four R's, not just three—Reading, Writing, Arithmetic, and Reality—the reality of the world, the global world that we live in.

In the military, about 44 percent of all service members are parents. The quality of education available to military children affects our overall readiness, it affects our retention, it affects the very morale of our force.

Service members consistently rate educational opportunities for their children as one of the most important factors in their career decisions and in deciding whether or not they stay in the military.

In equipping our military children with the best education, the best knowledge, the best skills that they need for the future, the Department is investing in its own future. Many of these young men and women will eventually follow in the tracks of their parents and will join the military themselves.

Education is also a national security priority, and for that reason we support efforts by the National Math and Science Initiative to build technical proficiency, and support expanding the instruction of critical foreign languages.

I have often said that when it comes to education there are four R's, not just three—Reading, Writing, Arithmetic, and Reality—the reality of the world, the global world that we live in, in which you damn well ought to have the language capability to understand that world, to understand the cultures we deal with, to understand where they're coming from. Frankly, one of the best things in dealing with the threats we confront is to understand who we're dealing with. And the ability to have language skills is truly important to that effort.

These efforts give young people a leg up in a complex and globalized world, and help develop a cadre of experts—such as engineers and linguists—that will in turn strengthen our force.

The bottom line is that our military is better able to defend the country when we address the long-term educational needs of those who serve and their children.

Since 2001, more than one million children have had to deal with the emotional stress and the extra responsibilities of having a parent deployed.

There are about 1.5 million school-aged military children, and more than 80 percent of them attend public schools in every state. These military-connected students learn a great deal from their parents' work, their parents' ethic, their parents' dedication to duty. Many of them travel the world at a young age, gain a deep appreciation for what public service is all about, and bring all of these traits and all of this wonderful, unique perspective to the classroom.

For these reasons, military children represent an enormous resource, enormous asset for educational communities.

They know better than most that their mom or dad—or both—serve so that the children in this country can have a better life, a more secure life. That is a tremendously powerful and positive message, but it also does not erase the hardships that these young people often must confront.

The Burden on Military Families

The past decade of war has placed a heavy burden on those who have served and it has placed a heavy burden on the children as well. Since 2001, more than one million children have had to deal with the emotional stress and the extra responsibilities of having a parent deployed, time and time again, to Iraq, to Afghanistan.

By the time military children finish high school, they will have moved an average of six to nine times, and twice during high school.

Each move, as we all know, means a transition to new friends, to a new school system, and potentially inconsistent academic opportunities and standards. This can pose particular challenges for the estimated 195,000 military children with special needs, as the quality and availability of service varies from school district to school district. It raises even greater challenges for these kids.

And of course, there are those students who have to endure the heartache of a Mom or Dad who never returns from the battlefield, or who returns alive to them but sometimes changed forever by the horror of war.

One thing that military parents should never have to sacrifice is the education of their children.

The toughest part of my job is to write notes to the families that have lost a loved one in battle—more importantly, to write a note to their children. It's tough to find the right words. The only thing I can say is that their loved one loved them, loved life, loved this nation, and gave their life for all they loved. And that makes them a hero forever in this country.

These sacrifices, large and small, take a toll on military children over time.

This hit home for one special operations soldier when he was at home celebrating his daughter's 18th birthday. He asked his daughter, innocently enough, when was the last time he was home for her birthday. She said, "Dad, when I was 10."

Our military families have to deal with many tough moments like that. They have to sacrifice a great deal for this country, and thank God that they're willing to do that. We have the best fighting men and women in the world. But one thing that military parents should never have to sacrifice is the education of their children.

This is why we all need to do more together to ensure that we meet the learning needs of our military families.

A Team Effort

The vast majority of our service members rely on local public school systems to meet their children's educational needs, and that means meeting those needs has to be a team effort.

Therefore, the Department continues to work collaboratively with the Department of Education, with states, with local school districts, and with organizations like the Military Child Education Coalition in order to ensure military-connected children receive an outstanding education.

But we cannot deliver on our commitments to these children without the active support, cooperation, and partnership of all stakeholders. I am deeply gratified by the significant progress that has been made over the past several years in deepening the cooperation and helping all military students receive the best possible education. It takes teachers, it takes counselors, it takes parents, it takes community leaders, all of them working together to make this happen.

For example, the Pentagon, together with federal, state, and local officials and administrators, and military family organizations, has developed an Interstate Compact on Educational Opportunity for Military Children.

That compact is designed to alleviate many of the school transition problems that are caused when a military family has to move from place to place, from base to base. It makes sure that transferring students are not disrupted by inconsistent policies in the areas of eligibility, enrollment, placement, and graduation.

That includes everything from immunization records to special education services, to extracurricular participation and course waivers.

Four years ago, 10 states had signed that compact. But as of this month, 43 states have done so, including most of the states with large numbers of military residents. That makes a great difference. I'd like to commend the State governors who signed on to the compact. Together, we must continue to push all states to adopt it, and we must make sure that states and local school systems are fully implementing the provisions.

We are working to strengthen and to modernize the Department of Defense's own school system, which serves about 86,000 students worldwide.

The Department has also expanded its partnership with local school districts, in an effort to provide stronger support to schools on or near military installations.

The Department of Defense Education Activity Partnership Grant Program supports outreach activities and provides grants that improve academic programs in military-connected school districts. So far, this program has awarded more than 140 three-year grants worth roughly $180 million.

These grants are providing an important infusion of resources to over nine hundred public schools that are serving

400,000 children from military families. This will enhance student learning opportunities, it will provide social and emotional support, and it will provide professional development for educators at military-connected public schools.

Schools on Military Bases

We are working to strengthen and to modernize the Department of Defense's own school system, which serves about 86,000 students worldwide.

My goal is to ensure that these schools remain a strong partner in sharing expertise and resources with local school systems around the country.

The Department is also actively working, in partnership with Congress and with local school districts, to improve the facilities of the 161 public schools on military installations. Through the "Public Schools on Military Installations" program, the Department is funding the maintenance, repair and revitalization of public school facilities on bases, while local education agencies match a share of that funding.

To date, Congress has appropriated a total of $500 million with the aim of helping to address the most urgent deficiencies. It's been my experience that if a school is not a proper facility, doesn't have the proper atmosphere, doesn't have the proper supplies and the proper equipment to do a good job, it makes it a hell of a lot tougher to provide a decent education. Today, I am pleased to announce that a total of nearly $60 million in grants have been awarded for 3 schools across the country, including an elementary school at Fort Bliss here in Texas, as well as two schools at Joint Base Lewis-McChord in Washington state to improve their facilities.

We will award additional grants this summer as part of our continuing effort to address capacity or facility condition deficiencies. We're going to do that at an estimated 21 public schools located on military bases.

I want you to know that the Department of Defense has listened. It's not always easy to get that big bureaucracy to listen but we have listened—listened to school districts, listened to organizations, listened to parents—and we will continue to listen to you. We will continue to fight to give our military children the very best educational opportunities.

This is and it must remain a team effort, and I am deeply appreciative to the Military Child Education Coalition, and all of you, for being such important members of this team.

We truly are one family in the military community. We have to be a family and we've got to hold each other's hands because it is extremely important that as a family we take care of our family members. Our men and women fight and sacrifice and die so that their children can have a better life and a better future. And I want to be sure that all of us will fight as well to deliver on that promise for them, the promise for their children, and for this country.

There's a story I often tell that makes the point of the rabbi and the priest who decided they would get to know each other so that they could understand each other's religions. They would go to events together in order to be able to use that opportunity to talk about their religions. So one night they went to a boxing match and just before the bell rang, one of the boxers made the sign of the cross and the rabbi nudged the priest and said, "What does that mean?" The priest said "It doesn't mean a damn thing if he can't fight." Now ladies and gentlemen, we bless ourselves with the hope that everything is going to be fine in this country. But very frankly, it doesn't mean a damn thing unless we're willing to fight for it.

You, by virtue of your presence here, have made very clear that you are willing to fight—fight to improve the education of our children, fight to help our military families and give them the support they need, fight to make sure our children have that better life, and I guess most importantly fight to make sure that we always protect and strengthen a government by and for the people.

Thank you very much and God bless all of you.

The Federal Government Advocates Making Occupational Licenses Portable Across State Lines

Janice Eberly and Jo Ann Rooney

Janice Eberly is the US assistant secretary of the treasury for economic policy. Jo Ann Rooney is the acting US under secretary of defense for personnel and readiness.

Military spouses not only play an enormous role in supporting our armed forces, but they also endure recurring absences of their service member spouse, frequent relocations, and extended periods of single-parenting and isolation from friends and family. Research suggests that the effects of these challenging circumstances can be mitigated by employment. Unfortunately, military spouses earn less than their civilian counterparts and are less likely to be employed, on average. A RAND study found that nearly two-thirds of military spouses felt that being a military spouse negatively affected their opportunity to work because of the "frequent and disruptive moves" associated with a military lifestyle.

Research on military spouses finds that employment positively affects their general well-being—both directly and indirectly. Specifically, satisfaction with career development prospects has a direct and statistically significant effect on military spouses' well-being. However, many military spouses are not satisfied with their career prospects. One military spouse said, "as time passes and I am unable to find work, my career dies and I feel like I have to abandon my personal and professional

Janice Eberly and Jo Ann Rooney, *Supporting Our Military Families: Best Practices for Streamlining Occupational Licensing Across State Lines*, United States Department of Treasury and Defense, February 15, 2012.

goals because my spouse is [in the] military." Although many military families depend on two incomes, they often face difficulties in career maintenance: "having to leave an excellent job behind, be unemployed for months, then underemployed . . . all of this affects our family's finances."

Military spouse employment and the associated financial and personal well-being is also an important component of the retention of service members. More than half of all active duty military personnel are married, and 91 percent of employed military spouses indicated that they wanted to work and/or needed to work. Research suggests that spouse dissatisfaction with the ability to pursue career objectives may hinder re-enlistment. Not only are military spouses highly influential regarding re-enlistment decisions, but more than two-thirds of married service members reported that their decision to re-enlist was largely or moderately affected by their spouses' career prospects.

Ensuring that licensing procedures do not needlessly hinder military spouses is critically important.

Difficulty of State Occupational Licensing

Complicated state occupational licensing requirements contribute to the difficulties that spouses of military personnel face in the workforce. State licensing and certification requirements are intended to ensure that practitioners meet a minimum level of competency and to help "protect the public from unqualified providers." Because each state sets its own licensing requirements, these requirements often vary across state lines. Consequently, the lack of license portability—the ability to transfer an existing license to a new state with minimal requirements—can impose significant administrative and financial burdens on licensed professionals when they move across state lines. Because nearly 35 percent of military spouses work in licensed or certified professions and are 10 times as likely to move across state lines than their civilian counterparts, military spouses are more frequently affected by the lengthy background checks, exams, fees, and other burdens associated with the lack of licensing portability.

> *DoD and independent studies have consistently found that "licensure by endorsement" significantly eases the process of transferring a license from one state to another.*

Military spouses have expressed their frustration with the lack of licensing portability. According to a May 2010 survey of military spouses conducted by Blue Star Families, a military family support group, almost half of respondents felt that being a military spouse negatively affected their ability to pursue a career, while one in five respondents cited difficulties arising from the lack of licensing portability. One military spouse said, "moving from one state to another, with different licensing requirements, has been a challenge. My career, while fairly portable, has still been difficult to maintain." Another military spouse, a real estate broker, explained the challenges of transferring licenses when she and her husband moved across state lines:

> I was a real estate broker in North Carolina when I met my husband. When we [moved] to Texas, my license was no longer valid . . . In order to reinstate my license, I would have had to attend Texas real estate school and pay Texas licensure fees. The cost to get my license and restart my business would have been more than I could have earned in the 18 months we lived there before [moving] to Kentucky. In Kentucky, I would have had to do it all over again.

Given the volunteer nature of our military, the sacrifices military families make for this country, and the importance of retaining these families to maintain the readiness of our military, ensuring that licensing procedures do not needlessly hinder military spouses is critically important. . . .

Best Practices to Facilitate Licensure Portability

DoD [the Department of Defense] has identified best practices that states could adopt to facilitate license portability. Although DoD initially focused on promoting specific national compacts and national certifications for two career areas (teachers and nurses), the Department has recently shifted to initiatives easing the overall licensing process in a state to affect a broader population of licensed military spouses. The Nurse Licensure Compact, which gives nurses a more streamlined approach to transferring a current license to a member state, provided DoD the key concepts (temporary licenses and endorsements) to use with states for expediting licensure in other occupations, particularly if the state boards adopt methods that can expedite the application and approval process.

Licensure by Endorsement DoD and independent studies have consistently found that "licensure by endorsement" significantly eases the process of transferring a license from one state to another. Standard "licensure through examination" requires the applicant to go through numerous state reviews in addition to passing national or state examinations and may include a supervised practicum or apprenticeship. Licensure by endorsement streamlines the application and state verification process for applicants with active out-of-state licenses, helping licensed military spouse professionals return to work more quickly. Obtaining a license by endorsement usually only requires that the license from the previous state is based on requirements similar to those in the receiving state, and without a disciplinary record. However, in some cases, applicants must also show they have recently worked in the occupation (such as two out of the past four years) as a way of demonstrating current experience or proficiency. This latter requirement can pose a problem for military spouses who have been unable to practice due to assignment overseas or in other locations. If a spouse does not meet these requirements, they will, at a minimum, have to undergo further scrutiny than the endorsement process generally requires, and in some cases, go through the full "licensure through examination" process.

Temporary or Provisional Licensing Temporary or provisional licensure is another way to ease state-to-state transitions for military spouses. Typically, these licenses are valid for anywhere between 3 and 12 months. To apply, the applicant usually has to provide proof of a current license, obtain a background check, and submit an application and fee. These licenses allow applicants to be employed while they fulfill all of the requirements for a permanent license, including examinations or endorsement, applications, and additional fees. Typically, temporary or provisional licenses are managed separately by each occupational area within a state, as is true for the Nurse Licensure Compact. . . .

Expedited Application Processes Approximately half of the states use a regulatory agency, such as the Department of Regulatory Agencies, [DORA] while the others regulate through individual occupational boards and do not have an umbrella agency to expedite the application process. Different approaches were required to streamline the process in these states.

Through internal agreements with individual licensing boards, the Colorado Director of DORA has the authority to expedite the endorsement process by interceding to approve applications that fulfill the boards' criteria. Two states which do not have structures analogous to that in Colorado found other ways to expedite the application process:

- Montana provided an innovative approach in [House Bill] HB 94 that allows boards to approve an application (for an endorsement or temporary license) based on an affidavit stating that the information provided is true and accurate and that the necessary documentation is forthcoming. Boards review the documentation upon receipt and can take disciplinary action if there are discrepancies.

- Utah HB 384 allows their occupational boards to approve the use of out-of-state licenses for "*the spouse of an individual serving in the armed forces of the United States while the individual is stationed within this state, provided*:

  1. *the spouse holds a valid license to practice a regulated occupation or profession issued by any other state or jurisdiction recognized by the division; and*

  2. *the license is current and the spouse is in good standing in the state of licensure.*"

While the Utah provision is the most inclusive and least intrusive for a military spouse, DoD will monitor its implementation to see if out-of-state licenses are accepted by employers as equal in quality to in-state licenses. In developing expedited approaches that save military spouses time and money, DoD does not want to make licensure easier for military spouses to achieve at the expense of degrading their perceived value in their profession.

Family Readiness Groups Provide Support to Families of Military Unit Members

US Army Operation READY

Operation READY (Resources for Education About Deployment and You) is a training and information resource developed by the US Army.

The FRG [Family Readiness Group] is an organization of family members, volunteers, soldiers, and civilian employees belonging to a unit/organization who together provide an avenue of mutual support and assistance and a network of communication among the members, the chain of command, and community resources. Unit FRGs consist of all assigned and attached soldiers (married and single), their spouses, and children. This membership is automatic, and participation is voluntary. Extended families, fiancées, boy/girlfriends, retirees, DA [Department of the Army] civilians, and even interested community members can and should be included, as well.

The FRG mission is "to assist commanders in maintaining readiness of soldiers, families, and communities within the Army by promoting self-sufficiency, resiliency, and stability during peace and war."

Goals of the FRG

Based on the FRG mission statement, the FRG may fill many important roles, including:

- build soldier and family cohesion and morale;

- prepare soldiers and families for separation during deployments and, later, for the stresses of reunion;

The Army FRG Leader's Handbook, Operation Ready, United States Army.

- reduce soldier and family stress;

- reduce the commander's and other leaders' workloads;

- help soldiers focus on their mission during deployments;

- help families become more self-sufficient;

- provide an avenue for sharing timely, accurate information; and

- promote better use of post and community resources.

For spouses and family members, the FRG gives a sense of belonging to the unit and the Army community.

Many experienced soldiers and spouses firmly believe that FRGs are important. Consider the following facts, based on recent research by the Army Community and Family Support Center, about the Army family:

- The ratio of immediate family members to soldiers is about 60 to 40.

- About 60 percent of soldiers are married.

- The ratio of children to soldier-parents is about two to one.

- About 6 percent of soldier-parents are single.

- Single soldiers have families somewhere.

- Families help soldiers make career decisions.

- Finally, the single most important concern of soldiers is that their families will be taken care of, both during peace and deployments.

So, effective FRGs are important for soldiers and families. To create effective FRGs, the five essential ingredients—leadership, organization, training, fun activities, and communication—must be built into the unit FRGs. Of course, this is easier said than done, but it's a basic fact that must be embraced by every leader—both military and spouse—if soldiers and families are to be successful.

The FRG—What's in It for Us?

For spouses and family members, the FRG gives a sense of belonging to the unit and the Army community—the Army Family. It provides a way to develop friendships, share important information, obtain referrals to needed Army resources, and share moral support during unit deployments. For the long-term, involvement in FRG activities can foster more positive attitudes among Army families and provide a better understanding of military life, the unit, and its mission.

Successful FRG programs, combined with ample and available community resources, help the Army achieve its primary goals—including the all-important goal of attracting and retaining high-quality soldiers and families in the Army.

For soldiers, peace of mind—soldiers can be assured that their family members will be more self-sufficient and will have reliable and friendly support while they are deployed. This peace of mind can help soldiers focus on their work, perform better, relate better to other soldiers, and be safer while they're on a training or real-world mission.

For commanders, the unit FRG helps to lighten their workload, especially in the area of soldier and family readiness goals. The FRG can enhance camaraderie and unit readiness by promoting self-reliance and by helping soldiers and family members to identify closely with the unit.

For the military and civilian communities, a well-established FRG program can help forestall serious family problems (such as family violence, substance abuse, juvenile delinquency, child abuse, etc.) that weaken Army families and place heavy demands on community service agencies. FRGs refer family members to military or civilian community resources and help families develop coping skills and stronger family units. Effective FRGs also provide a positive environment for diverse cultures to thrive together and to truly become one Army family—an Army of One.

For the Army, successful FRG programs, combined with ample and available community resources, help the Army achieve its primary goals—including the all-important goal of attracting and retaining high-quality soldiers and families in the Army.

For the Army Family and society as a whole, peace of mind; togetherness; pride in ourselves as individuals, families, units, and a nation of diverse cultures; and confidence that our Army can promote a better and safer world. . . .

FRG Structure

By regulation, the unit commander is responsible for establishing and supporting the unit FRG. Ideally, family readiness is managed from the top, and commanders have unit family readiness performance goals they must meet. Clearly, they can't meet those goals alone; they must identify capable spouse leadership and delegate clear responsibilities and the authority that goes with them to the spouse volunteers. Military members should not be FRG leaders. Commanders should encourage participation by all unit soldiers and families in FRG activities, which is best accomplished in a friendly, informal setting. Face it—soldiers of all grades will want to belong and will want their families to participate if the FRG is relaxed, democratic, meaningful, and fun. Remember, soldiers neither need nor want "another army within the Army."

Often, but not always, the FRG leader is the commander's spouse because the commander believes his/her spouse can best relate to the family readiness goals. However, every commander should consider what is best for the unit, the soldiers, the families, and the mission. The commander must have clear family readiness goals and take the initiative to ensure that they are met or exceeded by helping spouse leaders build and run an effective FRG. . . .

The unit FRG structure is designed to promote communication of important information and to encourage contact and mutual support among soldiers and family members.

It is through this grassroots organization and its activities that family readiness and soldier-family cohesion takes place. . . .

Like caring leadership, fun FRG events are critical to the strength and longevity of the FRG.

With today's smaller Army, active and reserve units that train for and support warfighting and peacekeeping missions experience unprecedented turbulence and uncertainty. These soldiers, their families (both immediate and extended), and friends endure frequent separations during training and longer overseas missions. Therefore, all units and soldiers must achieve and maintain a high state of readiness, and so must the families. Building and nurturing strong, active FRGs— effective FRGs—is critical.

Experienced commanders and FRG leaders have learned that certain factors make FRGs effective and successful, all of which involve five essential ingredients. . . . The goal of an effective FRG can be achieved through active participation in the FRG and by infusing it with the five essential ingredients listed below (shown in italics):

- strong, caring *leadership*;

- effective *organization* in a positive, friendly environment;

- work, *train*, and play well together;

- plan and enjoy *fun activities*, and include everyone;

- *communicate* well and share timely, accurate information; and

- make Army units and families stronger.

Each member of the FRG—regardless of rank, gender, marital status, age, race, or religion—is important and can make valuable contributions to soldier and family readiness, morale, and cohesion. Max DePree, author of *Leadership Is an Art*, reminds us that "by ourselves, we suffer serious limitations. Together, we can create something wonderful." By employing the five essential ingredients in the FRG, together we can "create something wonderful" and accomplish our goals. . . .

Essential Ingredients of an FRG

A brief overview of how each essential ingredient works in an effective FRG is shown below:

- Caring leaders—soldiers and spouses who lead and serve their units and FRGs with great regard and affection for the soldiers and families. Their focus is on the needs of the members, unit family readiness goals, and the military mission. Leadership of the FRG is, by far, the most important single ingredient.

- Well organized—the FRG leader recruits and motivates capable spouse volunteers to help organize and lead the unit FRG. With their help, the leader organizes committees and work groups, who accomplish all the key tasks of an effective FRG.

- Well trained—all members (every soldier and family member) are trained at some level to understand the unit's mission and family readiness goals, and their roles in helping to meet them.

- Fun FRG events—astute leaders ensure that the unit family regularly plans and enjoys fun events together. In fact, every event of the FRG should be enjoyable or at least pleasant for all members. Like caring leadership, fun FRG events are critical to the strength and longevity of the FRG.

- Great communication—the commander and FRG leadership ensure that pertinent information and knowledge of essential post resources are passed on to all FRG members in a timely manner.

Revolving around the essential ingredients like numerous satellites, the key tasks of effective FRGs are the many services that capable volunteers perform for all the soldiers and families. The commander's soldier-family readiness goals should mesh well with these tasks and support the unit mission. These goals are expressed in the unit Family Readiness Plan, which is reviewed with the next higher commander and the FRG leader. When the plan is complete, the FRG leader and committee chairpersons focus on the key tasks, organize and train the volunteers to help with the tasks, and lead the work for the benefit of all members. The result, of course, is an effective FRG.

Military Morale, Welfare, and Recreation Programs Offer Leisure Activities to Military Families

Military OneSource

Military OneSource is a Department of Defense-funded program providing comprehensive information on every aspect of military life at no cost to active duty, guard and reserve service members, and their families.

Military Recreation, or Morale, Welfare, and Recreation (MWR) programs, promote active living through participation in recreation, fitness, sports, cultural arts, and other leisure pursuits. Active living builds positive self-esteem and esprit de corps—essential qualities for personal and professional success. Active living also leads to improved personal health and well-being and helps build resilience and strong military families.

MWR is a comprehensive network of support and leisure programs and services designed to improve the quality of life of service members, their families, and other eligible patrons. MWR consists of a wide range of programs and services from fitness and outdoor recreation to libraries and bowling centers. Available programs and services vary at each installation.

MWR goes by many names across the Department of Defense (DoD): Army Family and MWR (FMWR), Marine Corps Community Services (MCCS), Navy MWR, United States Air Force Services, and Coast Guard Morale, Well-Being, and Recreation. Regardless of the name, all provide service members and their families with a variety of recreational programs on and off the installation.

"Morale, Welfare and Education," Military OneSource. Reproduced by permission.

Available Programs

Although MWR programs may vary from installation to installation, general MWR programs include:

- *Fitness and sports.* Fitness and sports programs develop cardiovascular fitness, strength conditioning, and flexibility, and promote healthy lifestyles. These include: swimming; self-directed, unit level, or intramural sports and athletics; and sports programs above the intramural level that provide competitive events.

- *Library programs and information services.* The DoD MWR library activities support readiness and the military mission, professional and technical education and training, Internet access, transition and career assistance, relocation assistance, and leisure needs of the military community.

- *Recreation programs.* Recreation programs provide opportunities for social interaction, self-expression, leisure pursuits, and cultural and educational activities that appeal to all segments of the community. These can include: free admission movies; outdoor recreation programs; recreational classes such as sailing, skiing, kayaking, auto skills, and swimming; and arts and crafts and other special interest programs.

- *Leisure travel.* The DoD Information, Tickets, and Tours (ITT) program provides economical opportunities for service members and their families to satisfy their needs for national, regional, and local travel, tours, attractions, and events.

- *Recreational lodging.* Recreational lodging offers eligible patrons the opportunity to relax and enjoy their vacation at a premier location while providing significant savings to the service member in the process. Recre-

179

ational lodging allows patrons to rent cabins, trailers, chalets, cabanas, beach houses, cottages, or hook-ups in trailer/recreational vehicle (RV) parks. Additionally, Armed Forces Recreation Centers are resorts operated by one Service for all of the DoD Components' use for the primary purpose of providing rest and recreation activities.

- *Single service member programs.* These programs support the overall quality of life for single service members ages eighteen to twenty-five by offering exciting and diverse programs and services that appeal to this age group and by encouraging and assisting single service members in identifying and planning for recreational and leisure activities.

- *Revenue generating programs.* These programs generate enough income to cover most operating expenses so they receive very limited appropriated fund (APF) support. Typical programs include golf courses, food and beverage programs, bowling centers, and marinas.

- *Child care and youth programs.* Child care and youth programs provide a system of quality, available, and affordable programs and services for eligible children and youth from birth through eighteen years of age. Specific programs include the Child Development Program, Youth Activities, Family Child Care, School-Age Care, and child care resource and referral.

Eligibility

Eligibility for MWR programs and services is broken up into two categories: unlimited use and limited use.

- *Unlimited use.* Generally, uniformed service members and their families have unlimited access to MWR services and programs:

- service members on active duty

- members of the Resent Components (Ready Reserve and National Guard; Reservists in training)

- cadets of the Service Academies and Merchant Marine Cadets

- retired service members

- honorably discharged veterans with a 100 percent service-connected disability

- Medal of Honor recipients

- non-remarried surviving spouses and orphans of personnel who have died on active duty or in retired status, or who were married to the service member for twenty years while they were on active duty

- DoD and Coast Guard civilians stationed outside the United States

- *Limited use.* Limited use eligibility requirements are established by the installation commander subject to local demand and capacity. The following groups of people may have limited access to MWR programs and services, based on the local installation patron eligibility policy:

- DoD and Coast Guard civilians stationed inside the United States

- retired DoD civilians

- DoD contract personnel and technical representatives when working full-time on the installation.

The Military Services Offer Many Recreational Opportunities to Teens

US Air Force

Although this list comes from the US Air Force, the other American military services offer similar programs.

Air Force [AF] Services Child and Youth Programs offer a number of activities to educate, guide, and entertain the young. Programs are available throughout the year at installations throughout the world.

Air Force Teen Council: The Air Force Teen Council (AFTC) is a network of teens working to resolve issues and voice concerns to the highest levels of AF leadership on behalf of teens globally or worldwide. Teens who have the opportunity to brief Air Force leadership on their issues contribute to the well-being of Air Force families. By interacting with Air Force leadership in person, the teens learn more about being a visionary and strategic thinker; they no longer think in terms of my installation but of the Air Force as a whole.

Air Force FitFamily: FitFamily is an important component of the overall Air Force fitness and health initiative. Air Force Child/Youth Programs (CYP) and Fitness Centers have partnered to promote the importance of healthy lifestyle choices and encourage Air Force Families to be active together. The FitFamily website provides resources, ideas and goal setting tools to help Air Force Families be active, make healthy nutrition choices and have fun in an effort to promote overall wellness.

One Page At A Time: Air Force Child and Youth Programs (FMP) is pleased to offer guidance for the youth One Page at

Air Force Services Youth Programs, U.S. Air Force.

a Time Program. This program provides a structured self-improvement activity that supports children's education and leisure skills development.

Space, Aviation and More

Space Camp: The Air Force Space Camp (AFSC) is a residential 6-day program that shows youth ages 12–18 firsthand what it takes to be an astronaut. Activities include simulated Space Shuttle missions, training simulators, rocket building and launches, scientific experiments, and lectures on the past, present, and future of space exploration. The camp is held the last week of July. Participants are selected through a competitive application process.

Teen Aviation: Air Force Services' Aviation Camp is an awesome opportunity for teens to have a glimpse of life at the United States Air Force Academy. Aviation Camp is offered annually the first week in June. Flying in a Cessna 145 is just one of the highlights at this camp. Participants are selected through a competitive application process. Only teens entering their sophomore or junior year of high-school may apply.

The Air Force Services strives to provide youth with opportunities to enhance their community, job, leisure, physical, and cognitive skills development.

Family and Teen Talent Contest: As part of the Nell Buckley Performing Arts Series, AFPC/SVPY [Air Force Personnel Center Directorate of Services Child and Youth Programs], in conjunction with AFPC/SVPCE [Air Force Personnel Center Directorate of Services Entertainment Branch], conducts an annual Air Force Worldwide Family & Teen Talent Contest. This program reinforces creative expression and helps our youth gain a better appreciation of the performing arts. The base-level program also provides a positive family experience for the entire base population.

Youth Of the Year: Air Force Youth Programs are affiliated with the National Boys and Girls Clubs of America (BGCA). As affiliates, we participate in the BGCA premier youth recognition program, the Youth of the Year. The program begins annually with each base Youth Programs selecting a Youth of the Year. To compete locally, nominees submit personal essays and information packages describing their involvement with home and family, moral character, community, school, service to club, and life goals. If selected as the base Youth of the Year, the young person then competes at state level. Each state winner may have the opportunity to compete in regional competition. This year six military youth will have the opportunity to compete at the national level. All installation winners are recognized by Air Force Personnel Center, Directorate of Services, Child and Youth Programs.

The goal of the Creativity through Cooking Camp is to expand and assist youths' understanding of the nutritional value of food using USDA guidelines, and support sensible eating habits, while designing and preparing a meal.

Teen Leadership Camp: Air Force Personnel Center, Directorate of Services, Youth Programs is excited to offer the AF Teen Leadership Camp. The camp is been held at the University of Texas at San Antonio, 8–12 July 2013. Teens will engage in team building, classroom workshops, and leadership activities while experiencing college campus living.

Special Programs

The Air Force Services strives to provide youth with opportunities to enhance their community, job, leisure, physical, and cognitive skills development. As such, a variety of week-long camps and other special programs are offered at installation level.

4-H Clubs: 4-H'ers across the nation are responding to challenges every day in their communities and their world. 4-H is the nation's largest youth development organization with more than 6 million 4-H youth in urban neighborhoods, suburban schoolyards and rural farming communities. As the youth development program of the nation's 109 land-grant universities and the Cooperative Extension System, 4-H fosters an innovative, "learn by doing" approach with proven results.

Creativity through Cooking: The goal of the Creativity through Cooking Camp is to expand and assist youths' understanding of the nutritional value of food using USDA [US Department of Agriculture] guidelines, and support sensible eating habits, while designing and preparing a meal. . . .

Participants learn to prepare traditional US entrees that are tasty and nutritious including jambalaya, picnics, and a Southwestern fiesta. The program also focuses on the use of seasonal ingredients so participants will create salads, and prepare fresh fruit. The teaching curriculum includes: history, culture, selection of ingredients and a variety of cooking techniques.

The YES Program allows all certified and enrolled high school students to "bank" volunteer dollar credits toward their postsecondary education.

Sideline Sports: The goal of the Sideline Sports Camp is to expand and assist youths' understanding of non-traditional sports, improve physical fitness and develop an appreciation for those sports as a lifelong skill. Youth are instructed on and demonstrate the ability to successfully participate in a variety of non-traditional sports that are preselected by the Installation coordinator. Some of the sports offered through this camp are: Ultimate Frisbee, Water Polo, Badminton, Fencing,

Water-Polo, Team Handball, Lacrosse, Team Building, and Bocce Ball. Youth are also provided with team building activities.

Performing Arts: The Air Force Services Child and Youth Programs partner's with the Missoula Children's Theatre International Tour project. This opportunity provides military youth of all ages with the opportunity to participate in the performing arts. The goal of the Performing Arts Specialty Camp is to expand performing arts experiences and programs throughout the Child and Youth Program flight by offering hands-on experiences at select installations. Children and youth participate in a variety of performing arts to include: dance, drama and music. A focal point of the performing arts specialty camps is the introduction of support of participant interest in performing arts through rehearsals, workshops and up to two (2) public performances on the final day of training/camp.

America's Kids Run: America's Armed Forces Kids Run held annually in May is a running event for youth and adults. The program is designed for youth to have fun with their families and be introduced to the lifetime fitness activities of walking and running.

More Opportunities for Growth

Y.E.S. (Youth Employment Skills): The Youth Employment Skills (YES) is a youth volunteer/internship program funded by the Air Force Aid Society (AFAS) and jointly administered by AFAS and Air Force Airman and Family Services Flight. This program, being offered at select installations affords high school aged dependents of Active Duty Air Force members an opportunity to learn valuable work skills while having a positive impact on their base communities. Program participation incentives are in the form of dollar credits for grant funding. The YES Program allows all certified and enrolled high school students to "bank" volunteer dollar credits toward their postsecondary education/training at a rate of $4 per hour volunteered in an on-installation position. Students may accumulate as much as 250 hours during their high school education, for a potential $1000 (maximum). In addition, the participating installation Youth Program will "bank" base community credits at a rate of $2 for every hour volunteered per student, up to a maximum of $10,000 per program year. For purposes of this program, "program year" is defined as the 12 month period beginning 1 June through 31 May of each year. See your local Youth Programs Director for more information.

Operation Purple Camps: The National Military Family Association's Operation Purple camps are a time for having fun, making friends, and reminding military kids that they are the Nation's youngest heroes. The mission of the Operation Purple program is to empower military children and their families to develop and maintain healthy and connected relationships, in spite of the current military environment. They do this through a variety of means, including the healing and holistic aspect of the natural world. The program is joint or "purple"—and open to children and families of active duty, National Guard or Reserve service members from the Army, Navy, Air Force, Marine Corps, Coast Guard, or the Commissioned Corps of the US Public Health Service and NOAA [National Oceanic and Atmospheric Administration]. The Operation Purple program includes camps for teens, family retreats at the national parks, and camps geared to address the needs of children and families of our nations wounded service members.

State Camping Opportunities: Each year, funding is given through the 4-H Military Partnership and Operation Military Kids (OMK) grants to states who desire to offer camp opportunities to military youth. Locations, dates and age requirements vary.

Military HOMEFRONT: Military HOMEFRONT is the Department of Defense website for official Military Community and Family Policy (MC&FP) program information, policy and guidance designed to help troops and their families, leaders, and service providers. Whether you live the military lifestyle or support those who do, you'll find what you need!

Boys and Girls Clubs of America Programs

BGCA Programs: BGCA has had a long and proud partnership with the military. 460+ Military Youth Centers have benefited from this great partnership. All military youth centers worldwide are affiliated with BGCA. 530,000+ military youth served. BGCA has been our primary source of training for overseas professionals.

Keystone Clubs are the Boys & Girls Club Movement's most dynamic teen program. It affords Air Force teens an opportunity to gain valuable leadership and service experience. They conduct activities in three areas: academic success, career exploration and community service. The Taco Bell Foundation for Teens sponsors the Keystone Club program as part of a multi-year teen initiative; a strategic partnership between the Foundation and BGCA provides Clubs with the tools and resources to create a positive place for teens as well as for kids.

Torch Clubs are chartered small-group leadership and service clubs for Air Force youth ages 11–13. A Torch Club is a powerful vehicle through which Club staff can help meet the special character development needs of younger adolescents at a critical stage in their development. Torch Club members learn to elect officers and work together to implement activities in four areas: service to Club and community, education, health and fitness and social recreation.

Power Hour: Making Minutes Count helps Air Force youth ages 6–12 become more successful in school by providing homework help and tutoring and encouraging members to become self-directed learners. The program kit includes a guidebook for homework helpers and tutors and charts for tracking and rewarding participants' progress.

More Government Programs

Stop Bullying NOW!: The U.S. Dept. of Health & Human Services (HHS) Health Resources and Services Administration has a campaign called Stop Bullying Now, which offers advice to kids, parents, school officials and others about steps they can take to address bullying. The theme is "Take a Stand. Lend a Hand. Stop Bullying Now!" Their website has a page with games and cartoon webisodes to help kids learn about bullying and how to stop it. Another page was created especially for adults that includes resources about bullying awareness, prevention and intervention.

Free Tutoring Service: Get a tutor 24/7 when you sign up for tutor.com. The website offers free tutoring and homework help for military/dependents stationed anywhere in the world.

Military Kids Connect: The Department of Defense (DoD) launched a new website for children experiencing the challenges of military deployments.

The highly interactive website, www.MilitaryKidsConnect .org, was created by psychologists at DoD's National Center for Telehealth and Technology. It helps children of deployed parents cope with the stress, changing responsibilities, and concern for the safety of their parents.

The center, known as T2, developed the website with informative videos, educational tools, and engaging games and activities for three age groups: 6 to 8, 9 to 12 and 13 to 17. The site features monitored online social network forums for the groups to safely share their experiences with deployments.

MilitaryKidsConnect.org is the first DoD website to connect children in the widely separated active, reserve, and National Guard military communities.

The website has features that will help children, parents, and educators navigate the wide range of practical and emotional challenges military families must live with throughout the deployment cycle.

U.S. Small Business Administration: Did you know the U.S. Small Business Administration (SBA) has an entire section devoted to helping young entrepreneurs? "Young Entrepreneurs Essential Guide to Starting Your Own Business!" is a free online course offered by the SBA to help young entrepreneurs get started. The course is self-paced, easy to use, and take only 30 minutes to complete. . . .

High energy, high adventure, and high experience camps are planned across the United States from Alaska to Maine and from Colorado to Georgia as well as states in between.

Camps for Military Kids

OPERATION: MILITARY KIDS CAMPS: The Office of Secretary of Defense-Military Community and Family Policy partnered once again with Department of the Army to fund Operation: Military Kids [OMK] Camps across the country. These camps are offered to a variety of ages with a key focus being supporting youth throughout the deployment cycle. Typically, they are led by the 4-H program in each state in collaboration with their State OMK Team, of which many of our bases are a part.

CAMP CORRAL: In addition to these camping opportunities, Camp Corral offers a week of camp to youth of wounded or disabled service members and veterans. Ages range from 8–15 at nine locations across the country. Visit http://campcorral.org/ for more information and to register. . . .

Military Teen Adventure Camps: Spend time whitewater rafting, hiking, rock climbing, winter camping, skiing, backpacking, mountain biking, exploring the environment, running rope courses, geo-caching, or practicing wilderness survival skills. Participate in these activities with other military youth.

Military teens (14–18 years old) have an opportunity to participate in adventure camps. . . . These high energy, high adventure, and high experience camps are planned across the United States from Alaska to Maine and from Colorado to Georgia as well as states in between. There are even opportunities for military teens in Europe. This is the perfect chance for teens to experience the outdoors as never before!

Each camp offers a unique outdoor experience that allows youth to build leadership, self-confidence, and teamwork skills while participating in activities like camp cooking and archery. Funding is available to assist with transportation costs.

Camps for youth with special needs (mental, physical, and emotional) are also planned in California, Ohio, and New Hampshire. There is something for everyone!

Organizations to Contact

The editors have compiled the following list of organizations concerned with the issues debated in this book. The descriptions are derived from materials provided by the organizations. All have publications or information available for interested readers. The list was compiled on the date of publication of the present volume; the information provided here may change. Be aware that many organizations take several weeks or longer to respond to inquiries, so allow as much time as possible.

American Gold Star Mothers
2128 Leroy Place NW, Washington, DC 20008
(202) 265-0991
e-mail: goldstarmoms@yahoo.com
website: www.goldstarmoms.com

American Gold Star Mothers is a nonprofit membership organization for mothers who have lost a son or daughter in the military. It provides support and sponsors memorial programs and events at which the public is welcome. Its website contains organization news and information for mothers who wish to join.

Army OneSource
website: www.myarmyonesource.com

Army OneSource is an official Web portal providing important, credible, and up-to-date information in one location for soldiers and family members to access at any time of day, regardless of component or geographical location. It includes categories such as family programs and services; healthcare; soldier and family housing; child, youth, and school services; education, careers and libraries; and recreation and travel. It also offers the Army Virtual World, a tool through which geographically dispersed soldiers can use avatars to keep in touch with family members, friends, and programs within their Army community.

Army Reserve Family Programs

(866) 345-8248

e-mail: help@fortfamily.org

website: www.arfp.org

Army Reserve Family Programs is an official US Army website with information about a variety of programs for reservists such as Fort Family Outreach and Support, the Army Family Action Plan (AFAP), the Army Strong Community Center (ASCC), and Survivor Outreach Service (SOS). It offers live support 24/7 to connect soldiers and families with the right service at the right time.

Blue Star Families (BSF)

PO Box 322, Falls Church, VA   22040

(202) 630-2583

website: http://bluestarfam.org

Blue Star Families (BSF) is a leading nonprofit membership organization founded by military spouses to raise the awareness of the challenges of military family life with civilian communities and leaders. Its mission is to support, connect, and empower military families by serving as a bridge between families and support and service organizations that are striving to help make military life more sustainable.

Fisher House Foundation

111 Rockville Pike, Suite 420, Rockville, MD   20850

(888) 294-8560 • fax: (301) 294-8562

e-mail: info@fisherhouse.org

website: www.fisherhouse.org

Fisher Houses provide free accommodations for family members on the grounds of major military and Veterans Affairs (VA) medical centers nationwide, enabling them to be close to loved ones who are hospitalized for a combat injury, illness, or disease. The Fisher House Foundation also operates the Hero Miles Program, using donated frequent flyer miles to bring family members to the bedside of injured service members, and offers scholarships to the children and spouses of injured service members.

Gold Star Wives of America
PO Box 361986, Birmingham, AL   35236
(888) 751-6350
website: www.goldstarwives.org

Gold Star Wives is a nonprofit membership organization for people who whose spouses died while on active duty in the military services or as the result of a military service connected cause. It offers local chapters, support, memorial programs, and volunteer opportunities and works to improve and enhance the benefits widows and widowers receive. Among other features, its website contains legislation information and videos.

Military Child Education Coalition (MCEC)
909 Mountain Lion Circle, Harker Heights, TX   76548
(254) 953-1923 • fax: (254) 953-1925
e-mail: info@militarychild.org
website: www.militarychild.org

The Military Child Education Coalition (MCEC) is a membership organization that partners with the military services and many other organizations to ensure inclusive, quality educational experiences for all military-connected children affected by mobility, family separation, and transition. It offers articles and other resources for parents and students, as well as training programs for education professionals. Among the materials available on its website are scholarship information and the e-book *Everyone Serves*, a free handbook for family and friends of service members.

Military OneSource
(800) 342-9647
website: www.militaryonesource.mil

Military OneSource is a Department of Defense-funded program providing comprehensive information on every aspect of military life at no cost to active duty, guard, and reserve service members, and their families. The website includes, but is not limited to, information about deployment, reunion, relationship, grief, spouse employment and education, parenting and child care, and much more.

Miltary.com

website: www.military.com

Military.com is the nation's largest military and veteran membership organization, with ten million members. The "Spouse" section of its site contains numerous informative articles on topics such as military life, relocation, available benefits, spouse employment, childcare, and social opportunities, many of them written by military spouses for newcomers. There is also an advice column answering questions about individuals' problems. In addition, it offers information useful to all citizens on how the public can support the troops.

National Military Family Association (NMFA)
2500 N Van Dorn St., Suite 102, Alexandria, VA   22302-1601
(703) 931-6632 • fax: (703) 931-4600
e-mail: info@militaryfamily.org
website: www.militaryfamily.org

The National Military Family Association (NMFA) is the leading nonprofit organization focusing on issues important to military families. Its mission is to fight for benefits and programs that strengthen and protect uniformed services families and reflect the nation's respect for their service. Its website contains information about its military spouse scholarship program and Operation Purple camps for military children, as well as a number of downloadable publications, including toolkits for kids and for teens, plus the results of surveys revealing military families' needs and priorities.

Operation Military Kids (OMK)
Department of the Army, Attn: CYS Services, OMK
Fort Sam Houston, TX   78234-7588
e-mail: support@operationmilitarykids.org
website: www.operationmilitarykids.org

Operation Military Kids (OMK) is a US Army collaborative effort with America's communities to support children and youth impacted by deployment. OMK's goal is to connect military children and youth with local resources in order to achieve a sense of community support and enhance their well-being, and to achieve this it partners with the American Legion, 4-H Clubs, Boys and Girls Clubs of America, and the Military Child Education Coalition. Its website contains information about the many programs available, news articles, and personal stories.

SOFAR: Strategic Outreach to Families of All Reservists
1619 Massachusetts Ave. #25, Cambridge, MA   02238
(888) 278-0041
e-mail: help@sofar.org
website: www.sofarusa.org

SOFAR is a pro bono mental health project that provides free psychological support, psychotherapy, psychoeducation, and prevention services to extended family of reserve and National Guard deployed during the Global War on Terrorism from time of alert through the period of reunion and reintegration. Its website offers downloads of brochures such as "Helping Children and Youth Cope with the Deployment of a Parent in the Military Reserves" and "Talking to Children About War."

STOMP: Specialized Training of Military Parents
6316 S 12th St., Tacoma, WA   98465
(253) 565-2266 • fax: (253) 566-8052
website: www.stompproject.org

STOMP is a federally-funded parent training and information (PTI) center established to assist military families who have children with special education or health needs. A parent-directed project, it exists to empower military parents, individuals with disabilities, and service providers with knowledge, skills, and resources so that they may access services to create a collaborative environment for family and professional partnerships without regard to geographic location. Its website contains information about the services it provides.

US Army Morale, Welfare, and Recreation Programs (MWR)
website: www.armymwr.com

The Army family and morale, welfare, and recreation philosophy is that soldiers are entitled to the same quality of life as is afforded the society they are pledged to defend. Its mission is to create and maintain "First Choice" MWR products and services for America's Army, essential to a ready, self-reliant force. Its official website offers information and news about the Army's many family and morale, welfare, and recreation programs, plus guest blogs by soldiers and family members.

Bibliography

Books

American Bar Association	*The American Bar Association Legal Guide for Military Families: Everything You Need to Know about Family Law, Estate Planning, and the Servicemembers Civil Relief Act.* New York: Random House, 2013.
Ron Avi Astor et al.	*The Military Family's Parent Guide for Supporting Your Child in School.* New York: Teachers College Press, 2012.
Ron Avi Astor et al.	*The Teacher's Guide for Supporting Students from Military Families.* New York: Teachers College Press, 2012.
Armin A. Brott	*The Military Father: A Hands-on Guide for Deployed Dads.* New York: Abbeville Press, 2009.
Alison Buckholtz	*Standing By: The Making of an American Military Family in a Time of War.* New York: Tarcher, 2013.
Anita Chandra et al.	*Views from the Homefront: The Experiences of Youth and Spouses from Military Families.* Santa Monica, CA: Rand Corporation, 2011.
Lorie T. DeCarvalho and Julia M. Whealin	*Healing Stress in Military Families: Eight Steps to Wellness.* Hoboken, NJ: Wiley, 2012.

R. Blaine Everson and Charles R. Figley, eds. — *Families Under Fire: Systemic Therapy with Military Families.* New York: Routledge, 2010.

Charles W. Hoge — *Once a Warrior—Always a Warrior: Navigating the Transition from Combat to Home.* Guildford, CT: Globe Pequot Press, 2010.

Cheryl Lawhorne-Scott and Don Philpott — *Military Mental Health Care: A Guide for Service Members, Veterans, Families, and Community.* Lanham, MD: Rowman & Littlefield, 2013.

Heather Means — *My Special Force: The Warrior Who Taught Me the Meaning of Life and Love.* New York: February Books, 2013.

Karen Petty — *Deployment: Strategies for Working with Kids in Military Families.* St. Paul, MN: Redleaf Press, 2009.

Michael J.R. Schindler — *Operation Military Family: How Military Couples Are Fighting to Preserve Their Marriages.* Lake Placid, NY: Aviva Publishing, 2011.

Michelle D. Sherman — *My Story: Blogs by Four Military Teens.* Edina, MN: Beaver's Pond Press. 2009.

Sarah Smiley — *Dinner with the Smileys: One Military Family, One Year of Heroes, and Lessons for a Lifetime.* New York: Hyperion, 2012.

Shellie
Vendevoorde

Separated By Duty, United In Love: Guide to Long Distance Relationships for Military Couples. New York: Citadel, 2010.

Marshele Carter Waddell and Kelly K. Orr

Wounded Warrior, Wounded Home: Hope and Healing for Families Living with PTSD and TBI. Grand Rapids, MI: Revell, 2013.

Mary Edwards Wertsch

Military Brats: Legacies of Childhood Inside the Fortress. St. Louis, MO: Brightwell Publishing, 2011.

Leah Wizelman

When the War Never Ends: The Voices of Military Members with PTSD and Their Families. Lanham, MD: Rowman & Littlefield, 2011.

Periodicals and Internet Resources

Fred W. Baker

"Chairman Links Family Readiness to Military Readiness," American Forces Press Services, July 21, 2008. www.defense.gov.

Vann Baker

"What Is a Military Brat?" *Military Brat Life.* www.militarybratlife.com.

Molly Blake

"For Military Spouses, the Hard Road Between Careers and Family," *New York Times* blog, July 24, 2012. http://atwar.blogs.nytimes.com.

Amy Bushatz

"An Open Letter to Military Benefits Haters," *SpouseBUZZ*, June 4, 2013. http://spousebuzz.com.

James Carafano   "Helping Military Families Deal with Grief," *Washington Examiner*, August 19, 2012. http://washingtonexaminer .com.

Anita Chandra et al.   "Children on the Homefront: The Experience of Children from Military Families," *Pediatrics*, January 2010. http://pediatrics.aappublications.org.

Andrew Cohen   "Quietly, U.S. Moves to Block Lawsuits by Military Families," *The Atlantic*, January 30, 2012. www.theatlantic.com.

Donya Curry   "Study: Military Deployment Can Weigh Heavily on Children, Teens," *The Nation's Health*, January 2012.

Beth Ellen Davis et al.   "Military Children, Families, and Communities: Supporting Those Who Serve," *Pediatrics*, February 2012. http://pediatrics .aappublications.org.

Jessica Dickler   "Military Families Face Financial Hurdles," *CNN Money*, March 27, 2012. http://money.cnn.com.

Glenda Fauntleroy   "Parents' Military Deployments Take Emotional Toll on Teens," Center for Advancing Health, July 26, 2011. www.cfah.org.

Karen Santiano Francis   "Thanks of a Grateful Nation? Military Families Say Not So Much!" The Broad Side, June 5, 2013. www.the-broad-side.com.

Claire Gordon	"11 Things Not to Say to a Military Spouse," *AOL's Homepage for Heroes*, October 18, 2012. http://jobs.aol.com.
Rick Hampson	"Holly Petraeus Makes Her Own Mark on the Military," *USA Today*, March 19, 2012. http://usatoday.com.
Molly Hennessy-Fiske	"Carrying Someone Else's Dream," *Los Angeles Times*, March 11, 2009. www.latimes.com.
Karen (blogger)	"Lifestyles of the Rich and Camouflaged," *And Then We Laughed*, March 12, 2013. http://andthenwelaughed.wordpress.com.
Sullivan Laramie	"Family Readiness Officer Finds Joy in Helping Others," Defense Video & Imagery Distribution System, May 16, 2013. www.dvidshub.net.
Maryann Makekau	"Giving Military Kids a Voice," *Time*, November 6, 2012. http://nation.time.com.
Sarah O. Meadows	"Military Families: What We Know And What We Don't Know," *NCFR Report Magazine*, Spring 2012. www.ncfr.org.
Katie Miller	"Collateral Damage: How the Defense of Marriage Act Harms the Troops and Undermines the U.S. Military," Center for American Progress, February 21, 2013. www.americanprogress.org.

Jeffrey Moody — "Military Children Are Resilient," Military.com.

National Military Family Association — "10 Things Military Teens Want You to Know," 2008. www.militaryfamily.org.

National Military Family Association — "We Serve Too: A Toolkit About Military Teens," 2010. www.militaryfamily.org.

Kathy Roth-Douquet — "Politics vs. Military Families," *USA Today*, February 26, 2013. www.usatoday.com.

Rebekah Sanderlin — "Finding Home Again After Deployment," *New York Times* blog, November 13, 2012. http://atwar.blogs.nytimes.com.

Amy Sciotti — "A Marine's Mom Writes," *New York Times* blog, May 26, 2012. http://atwar.blogs.nytimes.com.

Benjamin S. Siegel and Beth Ellen Davis — "Health and Mental Health Needs of Children in US Military Families," *Pediatrics*, June 2013. http://pediatrics.aappublications.org.

Fianna Sogomonyan and Janice L. Cooper — "Trauma Faced by Children of Military Families: What Every Policymaker Should Know," National Center for Children in Poverty, May 2010. www.nccp.org.

StopForeclosure Fraud.com   "Top Democrats Introduce Legislation to Protect Military Families from Foreclosure," May 7, 2013. http://stopforeclosurefraud .com.

Heather Sweeny   "A Spouse Confronts the Military-Civilian Divide," *New York Times* blog, July 8, 2011. http:// atwar.blogs.nytimes.com.

US Department of Defense   "Extending Benefits to Same-Sex Domestic Partners of Military Members," February 11, 2012. www.defense.gov.

US Department of Defense   "2011 Demographics Profile of the Military Community," November 2012. www.militaryonesource.mil.

Bill Webster   "Booming Military Benefits," *Washington Post*, June 2, 2013. www.washingtonpost.com.

The White House   *Report of the Eleventh Quadrennial Review of Military Compensation*, June 2012. http://militarypay .defense.gov.

Index